# QUILTS

## FOR CHOCOLATE LOVERS

*Janet Jones Worley*

**American Quilter's Society**

P. O. Box 3290 • Paducah, KY 42002-3290
e-mail: www.AQSquilt.com

Located in Paducah, Kentucky, the American Quilter's Society (AQS) is dedicated to promoting the accomplishments of today's quilters. Through its publications and events, AQS strives to honor today's quilt-makers and their work and to inspire future creativity and innovation in quiltmaking.

EDITOR: MARJORIE L. RUSSELL
GRAPHIC DESIGN: ELAINE WILSON
COVER DESIGN: MICHAEL BUCKINGHAM
PHOTOGRAPHY: CHARLES R. LYNCH

**Library of Congress Cataloging-in-Publication Data**
Worley, Janet Jones.
    Quilts for chocolate lovers / by Janet Jones Worley.
    p. cm.
    ISBN 1-57432-760-7
    1. Quilting--Patterns. 2. Patchwork--Patterns. 3. Appliqué
--Patterns. 4. Cookery (Chocolate)      I. Title.
TT835.W68 2000
  746.46'041--dc21                            00-012524

Additional copies of this book may be ordered from the American Quilter's Society, PO Box 3290, Paducah, KY 42002-3290, or online at www.AQSquilt.com.

# Dedication

To my husband Michael, who walked into the house one day with a huge box and said, "Well, if you want to learn to quilt you'll need a sewing machine." Thank you for your unfailing support and encouragement.

To my grandmother, Sadie Swetchman, who will always live in my heart.

**MY HEART BELONGS TO CHOCOLATE**

# Acknowledgments

*This book would not have been possible without the support and encouragement of my family and friends. Thank you from the bottom of my heart.*

**My gratitude to**

... the wonderful manufacturers and people listed in the Resources section.

... Beth Hayes, editor of *McCall's Quilting, McCall's Quick Quilts,* and *Vintage Quilts* who first published one of my quilts and started me on the path.

... three special ladies who each pieced a quilt top for this book – Kelly Corbridge, Lucy Fazely, and Diana Hofmann. You made my designs shine!

... the wonderful recipes and support of Diana Hofmann, Lucy Fazely, Cathy Scovill, Kim Martin, Kat Norman, and Cora Lee Reagan.

... the editorial and production staff at the American Quilter's Society for proving that dreams really do come true – Marjorie Russell "editor extraordinaire," this would not have been possible without you; Barbara Smith, thank you, thank you, thank you; designer Elaine Wilson, I can't thank you enough for such beautiful work; cover designer, Michael Buckingham, the book's cover is "delicious"; and photographer, Charles R. Lynch, the photographs are wonderful.

... Lucy Fazely, quilt designer and teacher, for her constant support and gentle nudging.

... Laurette Koserowski, Jeanne Stauffer, and Sandra Hatch, editors of wonderful quilting magazines and books.

... the "nieces" for their inspiration, and all my students and the SBs who make teaching more fun than chocolate!

*"What you see before you, my friend, is the result of a lifetime of chocolate."*

*Katharine Hepburn*

# Contents

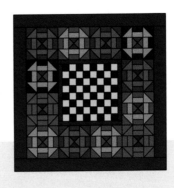

# Introduction

In the seventeenth century, King Louis XIV of France and his Spanish bride, Princess Maria Theresa, brought the fashion for chocolate to full flower. Louis granted a Paris merchant the first commercial license as a purveyor of chocolate. The secret was out!

Dear Quilter,

Chocolate. Doesn't the word just make you smile? I have never yet met a quilter who did not love chocolate. Pounds of chocolate have been found in almost every classroom where I have taught quilting. Quilters and chocolate just seem to go together.

I love chocolate and love quilting, therefore, this book was meant to be. Some of my friends developed the recipes in this book and I hope you will try them. I made the big sacrifice and sampled each recipe myself, so I know you are in for a treat!

If you are fairly new to quilting, relax and enjoy it. Like everything in life, the more you do it, the better you become. Great points and square blocks come with practice. If you meet someone who looks at you and says, "Of course all my blocks are perfectly square," yikes, run for your life and take the chocolate with you! The fabric, the weather, the thread – all will have an effect on your quilting. Do the best you can and then move on. Life is short and there are so many quilts to be made.

I have never yet made a perfect quilt and, to be honest, know that I never will. Take quilting lessons whenever possible but remember that those of us who teach have our own opinions. That doesn't mean one opinion is right and the other is wrong – it just means we are different!

I hope you enjoy making these quilts as much as I did. Just make sure you have your favorite chocolate on hand and let's have fun.

Quilt Long and Prosper,

Janet

# Basic Ingredients

*The basic ingredients of our favorite chocolate recipes determine the outcome of the finished product. The same holds true for the basics in quiltmaking.*

*This section contains the methods I prefer and hope you will enjoy. Remember there are no set rules in the art of quiltmaking. A method that works wonderfully for me may not be your cup of tea (or in our case, cup of hot chocolate). Try different methods until you find the one you like the best and gives you the best results.*

## Fabric

All the fabrics used in the quilts shown in this book are 100% cotton. If you have trouble choosing fabric, let the collections of various fabric manufacturers do the work for you. Each design line has many fabrics to choose from and they all work wonderfully together. So, no more pulling your hair out trying to decide if this color goes with that; if it is in the collection, the answer is yes! Now all you have to do is decide if you like it. That, to me, is the most important decision a quilter has to make. If you like what you see, that is all you need worry about. Your quilt must please you.

Before you begin, wash all the fabrics you select for these projects to ensure that your fabric won't shrink after the quilt is made. Damp iron and use sizing if desired.

## Appliqué

All the appliqué on projects in this book was done by sewing machine. I use fusible web and a zigzag or buttonhole stitch. The zigzag stitch is the easier of the two to use and corners well. I use a 1.5 width with a 1.0 length for most everything. When using the buttonhole stitch my setting is usually 1.5 for width and 2.25 for length. If your machine has different settings, practice stitching on scrap fabric until you find a stitch that pleases you.

The most important thing that I do in preparing for machine appliqué is to adjust the machine's tension. Almost every machine has an upper tension dial. The lower the number on the dial, the looser the tension. I always loosen the upper thread tension slightly so the top thread pulls a little to the wrong side of

**Fig. 1.**

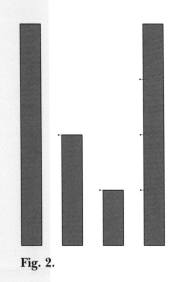

**Fig. 2.**

**Fig. 3.**

the fabric. This prevents bobbin thread from showing on the front side of the quilt.

Remember to secure the threads at the beginning and ending of your stitching line. Whether you are using a zigzag or buttonhole stitch, turn the stitch width to 0 and the stitch length almost as low as it will go. Make six or seven of these tiny stitches as close as possible to your appliqué piece before beginning your appliqué stitches.

### Borders

The way you measure and cut borders matters a great deal to the finished look of your quilt. When I first started quilting I never understood the reasoning behind all that measuring. I just slapped those borders down and trimmed off the extra at the end. "Why do extra work?" I always asked myself. Well, you do it because if you don't measure, your borders will ruffle like the ridges in potato chips. Now, while I love a salty ruffle chip, I don't want ruffles in my quilts.

To prevent the dreaded ruffle, measure through the center of your quilt from top to bottom (Fig. 1). This is very important since the edges of the quilt can stretch during piecing and one side may be longer than the other. So, measuring through the center is the most accurate.

Cut border strips for the left and right sides, piecing them together as necessary to make two pieces as long as the center measurement. Fold the border in half and mark the halfway point with a pin (Fig. 2). Fold it again, marking the quarter points with pins.

Fold the quilt top in half from side to side, inserting pins at the fold (Fig. 3). Fold it again and insert pins at the quarter points on either side (Fig. 4). Position the border on the edge of the quilt with right sides together. Match pins, pin together, and sew (Fig. 5). Gently press.

Measure the quilt top and attached side borders through the center from side to side (Fig. 6). Following the previous directions, cut a top and bottom border using this measurement, piecing as necessary. Fold and mark the half and quarter points with pins, position the border and quilt just as before, and sew.

The small amount of time it takes to accurately cut and measure your quilt's borders will be worth the extra effort in the long run. After all, ruffles should be in our potato chips, not in our quilts!

## Basting the Quilt Sandwich

Don't fear – all this talk of food is not fattening! A quilt sandwich is the quilt top, batting, and backing. The quilt backing must not have wrinkles or you will quilt those wrinkles into the quilt.

To prevent wrinkling, iron and then clamp the quilt backing onto a table using large office clamps. If you don't have a large table on which you can use clamps, you can tape the quilt backing to the floor with masking tape.

The next layer in a quilt sandwich is the batting. Use only good quality batting in all your quilts. Batting is like chocolate – the higher the quality, the better the product. It is important not to have wrinkles in the batting either. To remove wrinkles, tumble the batting in the dryer for 10 to 20 minutes on an air-only setting without heat. Then smooth the batting onto the backing and re-clamp the office clamps to hold the backing and batting secure.

**Fig. 4.**

**Fig. 5.**

**Fig. 6.**

*In merry ole London, chocolate houses became notorious gathering places for both the high and low of society. Rumor has it that England was where milk was first used in place of water while making the beverage, a suggestion that apparently came from Sir Hans Sloane, physician to Queen Anne.*

Now for the final layer, the quilt top. As before there can be no wrinkles. Also remember to snip any loose threads before positioning the quilt top on the sandwich. Smooth the top onto the batting and clamp as before.

Quilt sandwiches can be hand basted or pinned. Either way, always start in the middle of the quilt and work outward. I use pins most of the time. Be sure to use only 1 inch or number 1 safety pins; any larger and your sandwich layers will shift as you quilt causing puckers and those dreaded wrinkles!

Use plenty of pins, enough so that when you lay your closed fist on the quilt, it will touch a pin on the top, bottom, left, and right sides. Remember, more pins are better. As you quilt, just drop the pins into a plastic bowl without closing them. Why close them when the next time you use them they will need to be opened again? As you quilt, either by hand or machine, just remove the pins as you come to them. Happy quilting!

**Quilting**

Repeat after me, "My walking foot is my friend!" When I teach a machine quilting class, it always surprises me that more than half the class has never even taken their walking foot out of its packaging. I use mine so often that there have been times I thought I heard it groan.

The walking foot will keep all your quilts from getting the puckers. While your feed dogs are grabbing the quilt from underneath, the walking foot is grabbing the quilt top. This keeps the entire quilt flat and pucker free.

**Binding**

French binding is the most popular method of binding quilts. Binding strips can be cut in many widths depending on the type of batting used. I recommend bindings 2½" wide for use with cotton batting.

To make French binding, cut enough 2½" x 42" strips on the crosswise grain of the fabric to go around the entire quilt. Trim off the selvage edges and stitch the pieces together to make one long strip. Press the strip in half lengthwise with wrong sides together.

If you have an even-feed or walking foot for your sewing machine, use it to attach the binding. This type of presser foot prevents puckering while sewing through quilt layers.

Choose a point along one side of the quilt away from a corner. With right sides together, align the raw edge of the binding with the raw edge of the quilt. Leave approximately 6 inches or more of binding dangling free from the starting point.

Begin stitching the binding to the quilt top using a ¼" seam allowance. Stop stitching ¼" from each corner and backstitch (Fig. 7). Lift the needle out of the fabric.

Fold the binding up, perpendicular to the sewn binding (Fig. 8). Then fold the binding down again as shown, lining up the edges of the binding and quilt (Fig. 9).

Turn the quilt and position the needle at the seam line of the next side, ¼" from the top edge (Fig. 10). Make a couple of stitches, backstitch, and then continue stitching around the quilt.

Stop stitching approximately 6" from the beginning. Find the center point between the two binding pieces and mark it with a pin (Fig. 11). Lay both of the loose ends flat along the

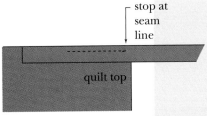

Backstitch to secure stitches.

**Fig. 7.**

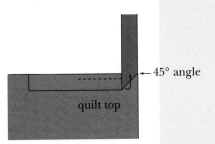

**Fig. 8.**

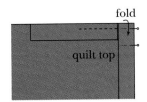

**Fig. 9.**

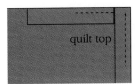

**Fig. 10.**

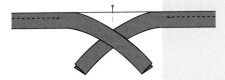

**Fig. 11.**

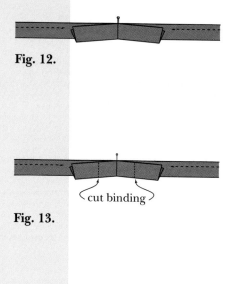

**Fig. 12.**

**Fig. 13.**

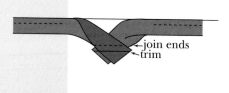

cut binding

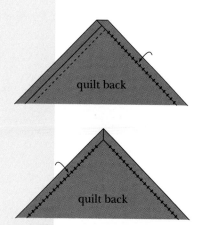

join ends
trim

**Fig. 14.**

quilt back

quilt back

**Fig. 15.**

quilt's edge. Fold the ends back on themselves and press to form a crease (Fig. 12). Trim the binding (Fig. 13).

Open the binding and sew the two ends together with right sides facing as shown in Fig. 14. Fold the binding closed, and finish sewing. Turn the binding to the back of the quilt and hand stitch in place (Fig. 15).

## Labels, or, How to Prevent Your Quilt from Being Wrapped Around a Refrigerator During a Move

Placing a label on the back of your quilt is very important. The more information you put on the label the better. No one can know all the work that went into a quilt without that information!

Nothing is more heartbreaking to a quilter than to see someone moving a refrigerator that is wrapped in a quilt. I have pondered this injustice and have come up with a plan. On a label on the back side of the quilt I'm going to include a picture of the person to whom I am giving my quilt, along with their name, date, and complete information about the quilt.

This may not completely stop them from dragging the quilt through the mud after I am dead and gone, but I think most people would hesitate before dragging their own face through the mud. To show you how serious I am about this, see the Resources section for photo-transfer materials.

# Quilt Projects

As you look through the projects in the following section, you'll be able to imagine what wonderful fun I had making and naming these quilts. You'll also see that the quilts are really not difficult to make.

Many quilters let fabric selection frighten them and give up before they begin. Here's an inside secret. The next time you're in your favorite quilt shop, choose a bolt of fabric that really appeals to you. Open the fabric and look along the selvage edge. Very often fabric manufactures print a row of colored circles on the selvage. Those little circles are your cheat sheet! Each dot of color is the perfect match for the bolt you have chosen. Selecting your fabrics is simply a matter of walking around the store selecting those colors. It's a simple dot-to-dot process.

Something else you might try is choosing your favorite chocolate cookie or chocolate dessert and thinking about the colors you could use in a quilt. Here's what I mean. Perhaps you like the colors of Oreo cookies but admire the design in the quilt STRAWBERRY CRÈME CENTERS, pg. 85. Well, the same design used in STRAWBERRY CRÈME CENTERS would make a great black and white quilt. Don't be afraid to dramatically change the colors of these quilts.

If I could have but one wish it would be that you have fun whenever you quilt. Don't let an unfinished project stop you from moving onto something new that really interests and excites you.

It pays not to take things too seriously. Just don't forget the chocolate!

Researchers at the University of California have found that chocolate carries high levels of chemicals known as phenolics, some of which are thought to help lower the risk of coronary heart disease.

Americans over the age of 18 consume 65% of the candy in the world (with age comes wisdom).

***THE FOURTH Picnic Throw, 48" x 56½".***

# The Fourth

What could be more American than rich chocolate cake brownies on the Fourth of July? This pattern includes a picnic throw to use while watching fireworks and a rich cake brownie that is easy to make. What a wonderful combination!

*Happy Fourth!*

Quilt Size: 48" x 56½"
Finished Block Size: 6" x 6"

## Fabric Requirements (based on 42" wide fabric)

| Fabric | Yardage | Pieces |
| --- | --- | --- |
| Navy star print | 2 yds. | |

**Alternate Blocks**
From 2 strips 6½" x 42"
    cut (12) 6½" squares.

**Setting Triangles**
From 1 strip 10" x 42"
    cut (4) 10" squares. Cut each
    twice on the diagonal.

**Corner Triangles**
Cut (2) 5½" squares.
    Cut each once diagonally.

**Outer Border**
Cut 5 strips 6½" x 42".

**Appliqué Pieces**
Cut 8 Template G
    8 Template H
    1 Template J
    1 Letter "U"

## Americana Cake Brownies

2 c. sugar
2 c. all purpose flour
2 sticks butter
¼ c. cocoa
1 c. water
½ c. milk
½ T. lemon juice
2 eggs
1 tsp. baking soda
2 tsp. vanilla
1 can chocolate frosting
1 pkg. Mini M & M's®

Preheat oven to 350°. Grease and flour a 12" x 16" pan. Place the butter, water, and cocoa into a small sauce pan and heat until the mixture begins to boil. While waiting for the mixture to come to a boil, place sugar and flour into a large mixing bowl. Add the lemon juice and slightly beaten eggs to the milk and set aside. As soon as the butter and cocoa mixture comes to a boil, slowly pour it into the bowl containing the flour and sugar. Mix together. Add milk containing lemon juice and eggs. Next add baking soda and vanilla; mix again. Bake for 20 minutes and let cool. Frost and sprinkle with miniature M & M's.

*In the seventh century AD, cocoa beans were a common currency throughout Central America.*

*1940.
M & M's were born!*

| Fabric | Yardage | Pieces |
|---|---|---|
| Red | 1 yd. | **Binding** |
| | | Cut 6 strips 2½" x 42". |
| | | **Appliqué Pieces** |
| | | Cut 8 Template A |
| | | 16 Template C |
| | | 8 Template D |
| | | 1 Letter "A" |
| Gold tone-on-tone | ½ yd. | **Inner Border** |
| | | Cut 5 strips 1½" x 42". |
| | | **Appliqué Pieces** |
| | | Cut 8 Template B |
| | | 1 Letter "S" |
| Gold print | ⅛ yd. or scraps | **Appliqué Pieces** |
| | | Cut 1 Template F |
| | | 13 Template E |
| Cream stripe | 1 yd. | **Background Squares** |
| | | From 3 strips 6½" x 42" cut (20) 6½" squares. |
| | | **Appliqué Pieces** |
| | | Cut 8 Template I |
| Fusible web | 1 yd. | **Appliqué Pieces** |
| | | Trace 8 Template A |
| | | 8 Template B |
| | | 16 Template C |
| | | 8 Template D |
| | | 13 Template E |
| | | 1 Template F |
| | | 8 Template G |
| | | 8 Template H |
| | | 8 Template I |
| | | 1 Letter "U" |
| | | 1 Letter "S" |
| | | 1 Letter "A" |
| | | 1 Template J |
| Backing | 3⅛ yds. | |
| Cotton batting | 52" x 61" | |
| Other materials | Navy 100% cotton thread | |
| | Rotary cutter, mat, and 6½"-wide ruler | |
| | Basic sewing supplies | |

Now that your pieces are cut, finish that brownie and let's piece some blocks!

**Fusible Web**

In the quantities listed above, trace templates and letters onto the paper side of fusible web, leaving ½" between pieces.

Cut the pieces apart, leaving about ¼" around the drawn lines. Following the manufacturer's directions, fuse the pieces to the wrong side of the appropriate fabrics.

Cut the pieces out of the fabrics on the drawn lines. Do not remove the paper backing until ready to fuse each piece in position.

After these pieces are fused in place on the blocks, they will be buttonhole stitched along the raw edge.

**Appliqué Blocks**

**1.** Finger-press each of the 6½" cream stripe squares diagonally in both directions. Use the folds as guides to help position fabric pieces.

**2.** Refer to a sawtooth block in the quilt picture and center a Template A piece on a cream stripe square. Remove the paper backing and gently fuse the piece in place.

**3.** Fuse a Template G piece in the center of the Template A piece. Then layer a Template B heart piece in the square and fuse it into position. Repeat, making a total of eight sawtooth blocks.

**4.** Once again using diagonal folds on a 6½" cream stripe square as a placement guide, refer to a flag block on the quilt picture. Fuse a Template I rectangle in position. Layer the remaining template pieces in this order: one Template H, two C Templates, one Template D, and one Template E. Gently press with an iron following the manufacturer's directions for fusible web. Repeat, making a total of eight flag blocks.

**5.** Again using the diagonal folds on a 6½" cream stripe square as a placement guide, center the Letter "U" piece and fuse it in place. Look at the quilt picture for placement of the Template F star and Template E star pieces.

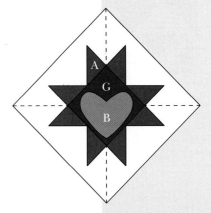

Placement guide.

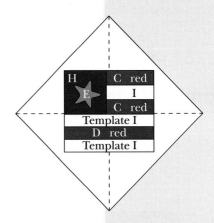

Placement guide. Template I will show through.

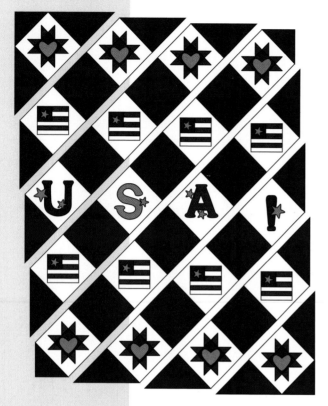

**Fig. 1.**

The Fourth
Template G

**6.** Center the Letter "S" piece on a 6½" cream square, and fuse one Template E star piece in position as shown in the quilt photo.

**7.** Center the Letter "A" on a cream stripe square, and add two E Templates as shown in the quilt photo. Fuse pieces in place.

**8.** On a 6½" cream square, center the Template J piece and add one Template E star. Fuse pieces in place.

**9.** Before the blocks are stitched into the quilt, buttonhole stitch around each appliqué piece, either by hand or by machine.

## Quilt Top Assembly

❧ Referring to the Quilt Assembly Diagram, Fig. 1, piece rows of cream stripe background and navy star print background blocks. Sew rows together. Add setting triangles and corner triangles as shown. (*Note:* Side and corner triangles are cut oversized. Quilt edges must be trimmed after assembly.)

❧ Gently press and trim edges.

## Borders

BORDER 1 – Follow the instructions on measuring and sewing borders on page 8. Attach the 1½" gold tone-on-tone strips to either side of the quilt, then to the top and bottom.

BORDER 2 – Attach 6½" navy star print strips to either side of the quilt top, then to the top and bottom. Gently press.

## Quilting and Finishing

Layer and baste the quilt top for the quilting method of your choice.

## Quilting Suggestion

This quilt was stitched-in-the-ditch around all the blocks and setting triangles. Outline quilting was done around all letters, hearts, and stars. Stars in a continuous line of quilting were used in the border and down through the navy star print blocks.

Bind quilt with red fabric following the instructions on pages 10.

The Fourth
Template B

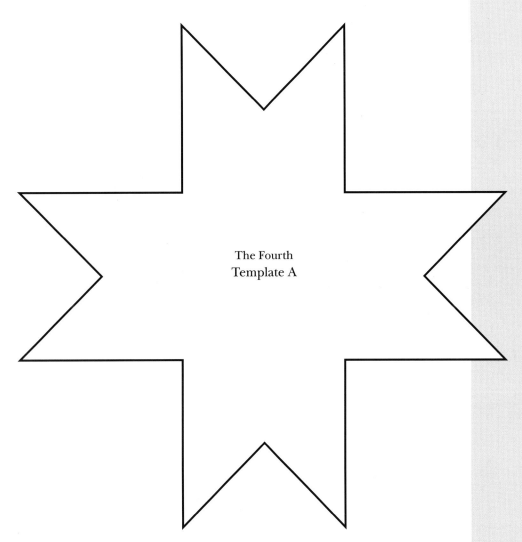

The Fourth
Template A

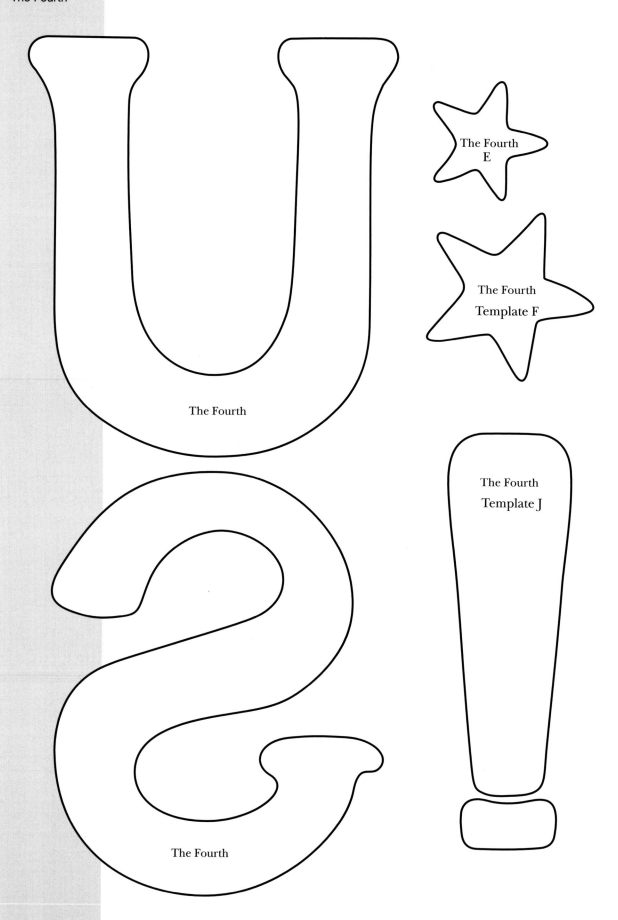

The Fourth

The Fourth
E

The Fourth

Template F

The Fourth

Template J

The Fourth

The Fourth

The Fourth
Template I

The Fourth
Template D

The Fourth
Template C

The Fourth
Template H

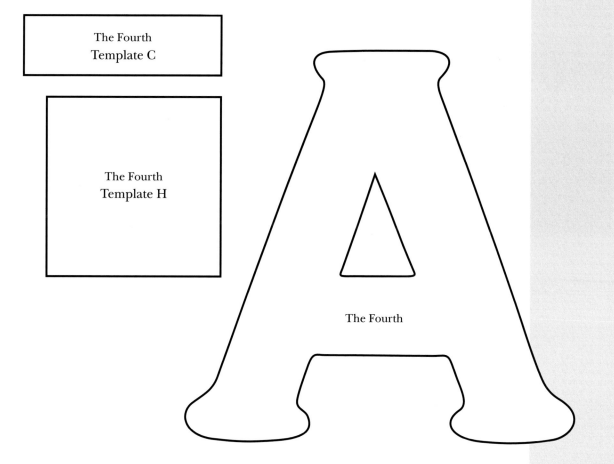

The Fourth

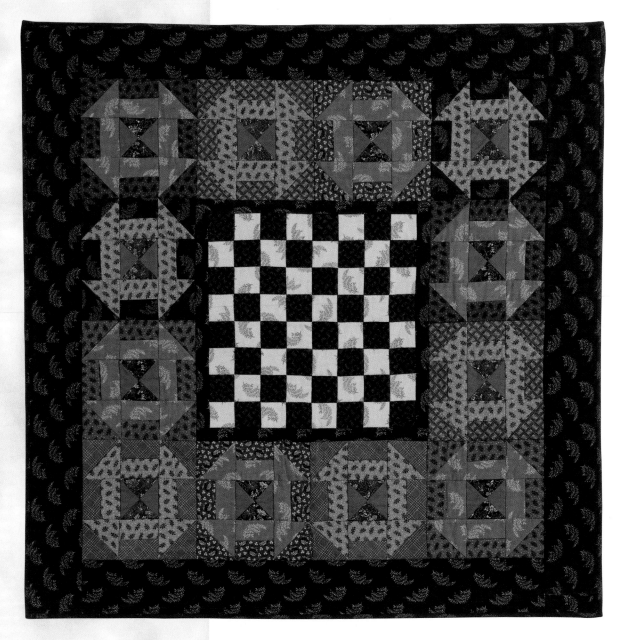

*HOT CHOCOLATE, 44" x 44".*

# Hot Chocolate

HOT CHOCOLATE *is a great lap quilt that can also be used as a game board for checkers! It was made with flannels to give it a special soft touch. This is a perfect gift for one of the men in your life. So make a steaming mug of hot chocolate and let the games begin. Just don't forget the marshmallows!*

Quilt Size: 44" x 44"
Block Size: 9" x 9"

*All fabrics used in HOT CHOCOLATE are flannels.*

## Fabric Requirements (based on 42" wide fabric)

| Fabric | Yardage | Pieces |
|---|---|---|
| Cream print | ¼ yd. | **Checkerboard Squares** Cut 2 strips 2½" x 42". |
| Dk. brown plaid | ¼ yd. | **Checkerboard Squares** Cut 2 strips 2½" x 42". |
| Tan print | ½ yd. | **Blocks – Half-square Triangles** From 2 strips 3⅞" x 42" cut (12) 3⅞" squares. Draw a diagonal line, corner to corner, on wrong side. **Blocks – Half-square Rectangles** From 2 strips 2" x 42" cut (24) 2" x 3½" rectangles. |

**Hot Chocolate**

    2 to 3 oz. milk chocolate
    1 tsp. butter (the real thing only)
    ¼ tsp. vanilla
    ½ c. cream
    ½ c. milk
    Miniature marshmallows

    Melt milk chocolate and butter over very low heat, stirring to blend. Add vanilla. Slowly add cream and milk. Top with marshmallows!

*"The superiority of chocolate, both for health and nourishment, will soon give it the same preference over tea and coffee in America which it has in Spain."*

*Thomas Jefferson 1785 letter to John Adams*

| Fabric | Yardage | Pieces |
|---|---|---|
| Beige print | ½ yd. | **Blocks – Half-square Triangles**<br>From 2 strips 3⅞" x 42"<br>  cut (12) 3⅞" squares. Draw a diagonal line, corner to corner, on wrong side.<br>**Blocks – Half-square Rectangles**<br>From 2 strips 2" x 42"<br>  cut (24) 2" x 3½" rectangles. |
| Six dark fabrics | ¼ yd. each | **Blocks – Half-square Triangles**<br>Cut (4) 3⅞" squares from each fabric.<br>**Blocks – Rectangles**<br>From each of six fabrics<br>  cut 1 strip 2" x 42"<br>  then (8) 2" x 3½" rectangles. |
| Burgundy print | ¼ yd. | **Blocks – Hourglass Quarter Squares**<br>Cut (3) 4¼" squares. Draw a diagonal line corner to corner, on wrong side. |
| Green print | ⅝ yd. | **Blocks – Hourglass Quarter Squares**<br>Cut (3) 4¼" squares. Draw a diagonal line, corner to corner, on wrong side.<br>**Binding**<br>Cut 5 strips 2½" x 42". |
| Brown | ¼ yd. | **Blocks – Hourglass Quarter Squares**<br>Cut (6) 4¼" squares. |
| Navy print | ⅞ yd. | **Inner Border**<br>Cut 2 strips 1½" x 42".<br>**Outside Border**<br>Cut 5 strips 4½" x 42". |
| Backing | 2¾ yds. | |
| Cotton batting | 47" x 47" | |
| Other materials | | Sewing and quilting thread<br>Rotary cutter, mat, and 6½"-wide ruler<br>Basic sewing supplies |

## Checkerboard Assembly

⑥ With right sides together, sew a 2½" strip of cream print to a 2½" strip of dark brown plaid (Fig. 1). Make two sets of strips. Press seam allowances to dark side.

⑥ Cut cream and brown plaid strips into 2½" units. Piece units into eight rows of four segments each, sewing dark to light fabrics.

⑥ To make the center checkerboard, sew the rows together, making certain that light and dark colors are next to each other. Gently press.

⑥ Inner border – Refer to instructions on page 8 for how to measure borders. Attach 1½" navy print border strips on either side of the center checkerboard, then to the top and bottom of the checkerboard. Gently press.

## Block Assembly

**1.** With right sides together, pair each of 12 tan print and beige print 3⅞" squares with one of the (24) 3⅞" squares cut from various dark fabrics. Sew ¼" on either side of the diagonal line (Fig. 2). Cut the pieces apart on the drawn line. Press open.

**2.** Piece together 24 tan 2" x 3½" rectangles and 24 dark print rectangles (Fig. 3). Piece together 24 beige print 2" x 3½" rectangles and 24 dark print rectangles. Press.

**3.** Hourglass centers – With right sides together, pair each marked green 4¼" square with a brown 4¼" square (Fig. 4). Sew ¼" on either side of the diagonal line. Cut apart on the drawn line. Press open to form a triangle square unit.

**4.** On the wrong side of one triangle-square unit, draw a line from the corner of the green

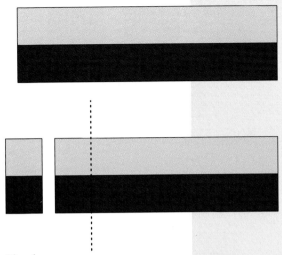

**Fig. 1.**

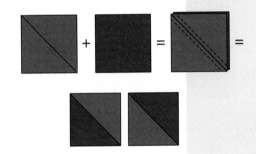

**Fig. 2.**

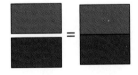

**Fig. 3.**

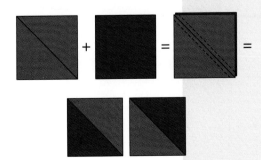

**Fig. 4.**

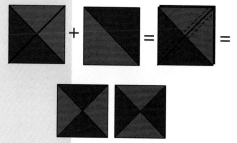

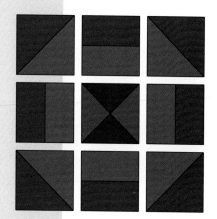

**Fig. 5.**

**Fig. 6.**

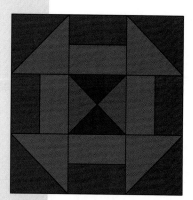

**Fig. 7.**

triangle to the corner of the brown triangle. Next, using another triangle-square unit of the same colors, position the two with the right sides of contrasting fabrics together. Sew ¼" on either side of the diagonal line. Cut apart on drawn line. Press open. You now have two hourglass squares for the center of your pieced blocks. Repeat, making a total of six green/brown hourglass squares as shown in Figure 5.

**5.** Repeat directions in Step 3, this time using burgundy 4¼" squares and the remaining brown 4¼" squares.

**6.** Block Assembly – Now it's time to assemble the blocks. Looking at the color photo of HOT CHOCOLATE, you can see that half the block sets have tan print with the burgundy/brown hourglass squares in the center and half have beige print with the green/brown hourglass squares. Below are the directions for making one block using the tan print units and the burgundy/dark brown hourglass.

**7.** Piece each block in horizontal rows first (Fig. 6), paying careful attention to the direction of the hourglass squares. (*Note:* I placed all mine with the brown fabric to the right and left of the hourglass.) Next sew the rows together as in Fig. 7. Gently press the block.

**8.** Follow the same procedure for making the six blocks with beige print and green/brown color combinations. Make a total of 12 blocks.

**Quilt Top Assembly**
❧ Follow the quilt assembly diagram (Fig. 8) to complete the quilt top.

❧ Gently press the entire quilt top.

## Borders

Attach the outer border following the directions on page 8 for measuring and attaching borders. Press gently.

## Quilting and Finishing

Layer the quilt top, batting, and backing in preparation for quilting.

## Quilting Suggestion

HOT CHOCOLATE was quilted using invisible thread and a walking foot. I quilted in the ditch over the entire quilt. On the border I quilted straight down the center all the way across all four sides. Since this quilt will be used as a game board and a lap quilt, I wanted it to lay very flat.

Bind the quilt with green fabric, following the directions on page 10.

*Anyone for a game of checkers?*

*Chocolate contains about the same amount of caffeine as is found in one cup of decaffeinated coffee.*

**Fig. 8.**

*LA CHOCOLADA!*, 49" x 59½".

# La Chocolada!

Next time you are in the mood for peanut brittle, give Diana Hofmann's La Chocolada Peanut Brittle recipe a try. This delicious peanut brittle has a dash of red peppers and is drizzled with chocolate. It is sure to make you dance the "La Chocolada" around the room, just like the dancers in the quilt's border fabric.

Quilt Size: 49" x 59½"
Block Size: 7½" x 7½"

*This quilt, like many others in this book, was made by selecting fabrics from a collection offered by a fabric manufacturer. These Robert Kaufman fabrics make the quilt, with zesty designs and spicy colors that give the finished quilt pizazz!*

## Fabric Requirements (based on 42" wide fabric)

| Fabric | Yardage | Pieces |
|---|---|---|
| Blue hats | 1 yd. | **Setting Triangles**<br>From 2 strips, 11⅞" x 42"<br>cut (5) 11⅞" squares.<br>Cut in half diagonally. |
| Blue dancers | 1½ yds. | **Border 3**<br>Cut 5 strips, 6½" x 42".<br>**Binding**<br>Cut 6 strips, 2½" x 42". |
| Black | 1 yd. | **Blocks – Half-square Triangles**<br>From 4 strips, 3⅞" x 42"<br>cut (36) 3⅞" squares. |

**La Chocolada Peanut Brittle**
(Recipe by Diana Hofmann)

    1½ tsp. baking soda
    1 tsp. water
    1 tsp. vanilla
    1½ c. sugar
    1 tsp. ground cinnamon
    ¼ tsp. ground cloves
    1 c. water
    1 c. light corn syrup
    3 T. butter
    1 lb. (16 oz.) shelled peanuts
    (unroasted or unsalted roasted
    will work)
    1 tsp. red pepper flakes
    ½ cup chocolate chip morsels
    Equipment: large saucepan, candy thermometer, wooden spoon, 1 large cookie sheet, 11" x 17".

    Butter cookie sheet and set aside. Heat oven to a low, warming temperature. Measure the soda, 1 teaspoon water, and vanilla into a small bowl. Mix well and set aside.

*(continued on page 30)*

La Chocolada!

Measure sugar, cinnamon, and cloves into a bowl and mix well. Combine this sugar mixture, the corn syrup, and 1 cup water in the saucepan. Stir together. Measure the butter, peanuts, and pepper flakes; set them aside.

Set up a candy thermometer according to the manufacturer's instructions and begin heating the sugar mixture on medium heat. Stay close and stir often to avoid scorching or burning the sugar. Warning: sugar syrup is very hot and it is not wise to leave it unattended, especially if children are present!

Continue to heat and stir the sugar mixture until it reaches the soft ball stage, 240°. At that temperature, add the butter, peanuts, and pepper flakes. Sprinkle the flakes as you add them to prevent them from clumping. Mix well.

Place your cookie sheet in the warm oven. Continue to stir the mixture periodically until it reaches a temperature of 300°, the hard crack stage. As the mixture nears the 300° mark, remove the cookie sheet from the oven and set it nearby. The warm cookie sheet will help keep the brittle from cooling too quickly, giving you more working time as you spread the mixture.

Once the mixture reaches 300°, remove the pan from the heat, remove the thermometer and add the soda, water, and vanilla mixture. Stir thoroughly. The soda causes carbonation. The resulting air bubbles make the mixture puff up and give it a light texture.

Pour the mixture onto the warm, buttered cookie sheet and spread it to a ¼" thickness with a wooden spoon. Allow the brittle to cool. Melt ½ cup chocolate chip morsels and drizzle over the brittle. Enjoy!

| Fabric | Yardage | Pieces |
|---|---|---|
| Black (cont.) | | **Blocks – Squares** |
| | | From 4 strips, 2" x 42" |
| | | cut (72) 2" squares. |
| | | **Border 2** |
| | | Cut 4 strips, 2" x 42". |
| Red | ⅜ yd. | **Blocks – Squares** |
| | | From 1 strip, 2" x 42" |
| | | cut (18) 2" squares. |
| | | **Blocks – Half-square Triangles** |
| | | From 2 strips, 2⅜" x 42" |
| | | cut (36) 2⅜" squares. |
| Gold | ¼ yd. | **Blocks – Half-square Triangles** |
| | | From 2 strips, 2⅜" x 42" |
| | | cut (36) 2⅜" squares. |
| | | Draw diagonal line, corner |
| | | to corner, on wrong side. |
| | | **Border 1** |
| | | Cut 4 strips, 1½" x 42". |
| 18 assorted fabrics | ⅛ yd. each | **Blocks – Half-square Triangles** |
| | | Cut (4) 3⅞" squares from each fabric. |
| | | Draw a diagonal line, corner |
| | | to corner, on wrong side. |
| Backing | 3⅛ yds. | |
| Cotton batting | 53" x 63½" | |
| Other materials | Thread | |
| | Rotary cutter, mat, and 6½"-wide ruler | |
| | Basic sewing supplies | |

## Block Assembly

**1.** To make small triangle half-square block pieces, pair 2⅜" gold squares with 2⅜" red squares, right sides together and drawn side up. Sew ¼" on either side of the diagonal line (Fig. 1). Cut the pieces apart on the drawn line. Press open.

**2.** To make large triangle half-square block pieces, pair each of the 3⅞" squares cut from 18 assorted fabrics with a 3⅞" black square, right sides together and drawn side up. Sew ¼" on either side of the diagonal line as shown in Fig. 1. Cut the pieces apart on the drawn line. Press open.

**3.** Begin piecing blocks by sewing the center strip in the sequence shown in Fig. 2. Make 18 center strips.

**4.** Piece together remaining small squares and half-square triangle units to make a total of 36 units (Fig. 3).

**4.** Sort large triangle half square blocks according to color. Attach two squares of the same color to the above units as shown in Fig. 4 to make a strip. Make 36 strips.

**5.** Attach two strips of the same color to a center strip as shown in Fig. 5 to make each block. Make a total of 18 blocks (Fig. 6, page 32).

### Quilt Top Assembly

⑥ The blocks in this quilt are set on point so the rows are pieced on the diagonal. Refer to the quilt photo for color placement. Sew together six rows of LA CHOCOLADA blocks and blue hat setting triangles (Fig. 7, page 32).

⑥ Sew rows together and attach blue hat corner triangles.

⑥ Gently press and trim quilt edges even.

### Borders

BORDER 1 – Sew gold 1½" border strips together. Follow the instructions on page 8 for how to measure and sew border. Sew gold borders on sides of quilt, then to the top and bottom of quilt.

BORDER 2 – Sew 2" black border strips together. Sew borders on sides of quilt, then to the top and bottom of the quilt.

BORDER 3 – Sew 6½" blue dancers outer border strips together and stitch to the sides of quilt and then to the top and bottom. Gently press quilt top.

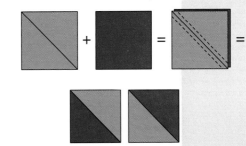

**Fig. 1.**

**Fig. 2.**

**Fig. 3.**

**Fig. 4.**

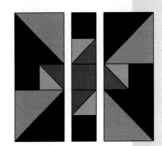

**Fig. 5.**

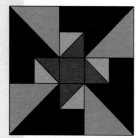

**Fig. 6.**

**Fig. 7.**

## Quilting and Finishing

Layer and baste the quilt top in preparation for the quilting method of your choice. Additional information is included on page 9 for basting the quilt.

## Quilting Suggestion

LA CHOCOLADA! was machine quilted in a large stipple or meander design as wide across as your index finger. The fabric is very bright and busy. It dominates so much that even if you used flowers or puppies as a quilting design it wouldn't matter. When using fabrics like these, I prefer a thread that will disappear. In this case, black thread was used. In many quilts I have used invisible thread with great results.

Sew blue dancer fabric binding pieces together. Follow the instructions on page 10 for attaching binding.

*CHOCOLATE COVERED CHERRIES, 55" x 73".*

# Chocolate Covered Cherries

Each year around Christmas, one of the first presents I buy is a box of chocolate covered cherries for my husband, Michael. They are his favorite.

CHOCOLATE COVERED CHERRIES is a very easy quilt to make. I hope you enjoy making it as much as Michael enjoys his chocolate covered cherries.

*Oregon has the only known chocolate fountain in the world! Two tons of chocolate flow night and day from a unique monument sculpted from marble and bronze.*

Quilt Size: 55" x 73"
Block Size: 11½" x 11½"

**Fabric Requirements** (based on 42" wide fabric)

| Fabric | Yardage | Pieces |
|---|---|---|
| Dk. brown/ pink print | 2⅜ yds. | **Border 3** |
| | | Cut 7 strips, 6½" x 42". |
| | | **Blocks – Checkerboard Squares** |
| | | Cut 3 strips, 1⅞" x 42". |
| | | **Blocks – Squares** |
| | | From 1 strip, 3¼" x 42" cut (8) 3¼" squares. |
| | | **Sashing Squares** |
| | | From 1 strip, 2" x 42" cut (17) 2" squares. |
| | | **Binding** |
| | | Cut 7 strips, 2½" x 42". |
| Hot pink print | ¼ yd. | **Blocks – Checkerboard Squares** |
| | | Cut 3 strips, 1⅞" x 42". |

| Fabric | Yardage | Pieces |
|---|---|---|
| Lt. pink print | 2 yds. | **Blocks – Half-square Triangles** |

From 6 strips, 2⅞" x 42"
   cut (80) 2⅞" squares.
Cut once diagonally.

**Blocks – Checkerboard Square**
**Corner Triangles**
From 2 strips, 4¾" x 42"
   cut (16) 4¾" squares.
Cut once diagonally.

**Setting Triangles**
From 1 strip, 17½" x 42"
   cut (2) 17½" squares.
Cut twice diagonally.

**Corner Triangles**
From 1 strip, 9" x 42"
   cut (2) 9" squares.
Cut twice diagonally.

**Border 2**
Cut 5 strips, 2" x 42".

| Fabric | Yardage | Pieces |
|---|---|---|
| Choc. brown | ½ yd. | **Blocks – Half-square Triangles** |

From 2 strips, 4¾" x 42"
   cut (16) 4¾" squares.
Cut once diagonally.

**Border 1**
Cut 5 strips, 2" x 42".

| Fabric | Yardage | Pieces |
|---|---|---|
| Tiger print | ⅝ yd. | **Sashing Strips** |

From 8 strips, 2" x 42"
   cut (24) 2" x 12" rectangles.

| Fabric | Yardage | |
|---|---|---|
| Backing | 4½ yds. | |
| Cotton batting | 59" x 77" | |
| Other materials | 100% cotton thread | |
| | Rotary cutter, mat, and 6½"-wide ruler | |
| | Basic sewing supplies | |

## Block Assembly

1. Referring to Fig. 1, page 36, with right sides together, sew each 1⅞" brown/pink print strip to a 1⅞" hot pink print strip. Cut pieced strips into (64) 1⅞" units.

2. Sew two units together as shown in Fig. 2, page 36. Make 32.

*Chocolate covered cherries were born in 1929 at Cella's Confections in New York.*

*Chocolate lovers will spend more than $300 million on boxed chocolates during the winter holidays.*

**Fig. 1.**

**3.** Sew light pink print triangles to each side of all segments as shown in Fig. 3.

**4.** Sew light pink print half-square triangles to chocolate brown half-square triangles (Fig. 4). Make 32 units.

**5.** Sew light pink print triangles to all sides of 3¼" brown/pink print squares (Fig. 5). Make eight units.

**6.** Referring to Fig. 6 for color arrangements, piece block units together as shown. Press seams.

**7.** Sew block strips together as shown to make eight blocks (Fig. 7). Press gently.

## Quilt Top Assembly

❧Sew tiger print sashing strips to each side of blocks as shown in Fig. 8.

❧Make the following sashing units by piecing 2" x 12" tiger print sashing pieces to 2" brown/pink sashing squares:

    2 – one strip units
    2 – three strip units
    1 – four strip unit

❧Each strip should begin and end with a square.

❧*Note:* This quilt is set on the diagonal, so the rows will be pieced on the diagonal as well.

❧Piece together two rows of three blocks each. Attach a setting triangle to the right side of one row of three blocks, and to the left side of the other as shown in Fig. 9.

❧Attach sashing strips as shown in Fig. 10, page 38, being sure to match seams. (The

**Fig. 2.**

**Fig. 3.**

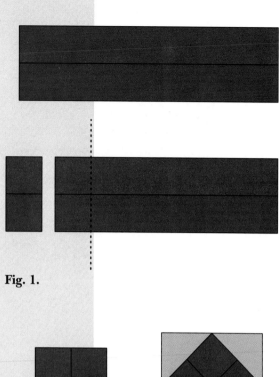
**Fig. 4.**
**Fig. 5.**

**Fig. 6.**

edges of the sashing squares will be trimmed off before borders are attached.) Add corner pieces as shown.

❻Press gently and trim edges. The rest is a piece of cake... or should I say candy?

## Borders

BORDER 1 – Referring to Quilt Assembly Diagram (Fig. 11, page 38) attach the first border. Follow the instructions on page 8 on how to measure, piece, and sew borders.

BORDER 2 – Follow by adding the light pink print border.

BORDER 3 – Attach the 6½" brown/pink outer border. Gently press the quilt top.

## Quilting and Finishing

Layer and baste the quilt top for the quilting method of your choice.

## Quilting Suggestion

When making a decision on quilting design, I always find that it helps to pin the completed quilt top to my design wall and view it from as far away as possible.

With CHOCOLATE COVERED CHERRIES, the fabrics dominate, and there is so much going on in the design. So I decided that only the simplest of quilting designs would work for this quilt. The overall meander, or scroll stipple, was done with medium brown thread. Another quilting option would have been stitching in the ditch.

Bind CHOCOLATE COVERED CHERRIES with brown/pink fabric.

Fig. 7.

Fig. 8.

Fig. 9.

**Fig. 10.**

*Question:*
*Is chocolate poison to dogs?*

*Answer:*
*It is not chocolate itself that is poison to dogs; rather, it is the chemical theobromine found in chocolate, tea, coffee, and cola. It can trigger epileptic seizures and can also cause cardiac irregularities!*

*Harvard researchers*
*have discovered*
*sweet-eaters live*
*longer!*

**Fig. 11.**

**CHOCOLATE POUND CAKE, 67" x 84".**

# Chocolate Pound Cake

*This quilt is very easy and can be made into any size you desire, just add rows until you get the size you need.*

*This pound cake is also easy and was developed by a dear quilting friend, Kathryn (Kat) Norman and her grandmother, Cora Lee. It is truly heavenly! Many thanks to them for sharing such a wonderful chocolate delight!*

**Mama Reagan's**
**Chocolate Pound Cake**

- ½ lb. butter (2 sticks)
- ¼ lb. margarine (1 stick)
- 3 c. sugar
- 5 eggs
- 3 c. plain flour
- ½ tsp. baking powder
- ½ tsp. salt
- 4 heaping T. cocoa
- 1 c. milk

Preheat oven to 300°. Cream butter, margarine, and sugar in a large mixing bowl. In a smaller bowl, beat eggs and milk together. Sift the dry ingredients into another small bowl or onto a large sheet of wax paper. Add some of the egg mixture to the sugar batter and mix well. Then add some of the flour mixture and mix well. Alternate adding mixtures until all the ingredients are combined to make a thick batter.

*(continued on page 41)*

Quilt Size: 67" x 84"
Finished Block Size: 12" x 12"

## Fabric Requirements (based on 42" wide fabric)

| Fabric | Yardage | Pieces |
|---|---|---|
| Cream | 3 yds. | **Blocks – Half-square Triangles** |

**Blocks – Half-square Triangles**
From 11 strips, 2⅞" x 42"
    cut (144) 2⅞" squares.
    Cut once diagonally.

**Blocks – Squares**
From 5 strips, 2½" x 42"
    cut (72) 2½" squares.

**Setting Triangles**
From 2 strips, 18¼" x 42"
    cut (3) 18¼" squares.
    Cut twice diagonally.

**Corner Triangles**
Cut (2) 9⅜" squares.
    Cut once diagonally.

| Fabric | Yardage | Pieces |
|---|---|---|
| Green | 1 yd. | **Blocks – Half-square Triangles** |
| | | From 6 strips, 2⅞" x 42" |
| | | cut (72) 2⅞" squares. |
| | | Cut once diagonally. |
| | | **Blocks – Squares** |
| | | From 5 strips, 2½" x 42" |
| | | cut (72) 2½" squares. |
| Brown | ¾ yd. | **Blocks – Rectangles** |
| | | From 5 strips, 4½" x 42" |
| | | cut (72) 2½" x 4½" rectangles. |
| Light blue | ⅜ yd. | **Blocks – Quarter-square Triangles** |
| | | From 3 strips, 5¼" x 42" |
| | | cut (72) 5¼" squares. |
| | | Cut twice diagonally. |
| Red | ⅞ yd. | **Blocks – Center Squares** |
| | | Cut 3 strips, 2½" x 42". |
| | | **Border 1** |
| | | Cut 7 strips, 2½" x 42". |
| Blue/brown | 2½ yds. | **Blocks – Center Squares** |
| | | Cut 3 strips, 2½" x 42". |
| | | **Border 2** |
| | | Cut 8 strips, 6½" x 42". |
| | | **Binding** |
| | | Cut 8 strips, 2½" x 42". |
| Backing | 5¼ yds. | |
| Cotton batting | 71" x 88" | |
| Other materials | Rotary cutter, mat, and 6½"-wide ruler | |
| | 100% cotton thread | |
| | Basic sewing supplies | |

## Block Assembly

1. Sew a cream 2⅞" triangle to the sides of each 5¼" light blue triangle as shown in Fig. 1, page 42. Make 72 units.

2. Sew remaining cream 2⅞" triangles to 2⅞" green triangles. Make a total of 144 units.

3. Sew a green 2½" square to either side of (36) 2½" x 4½" brown rectangles.

Using butter or shortening, grease a bundt cake pan. Instead of flouring the pan, try Cora Lee Reagan's trick and dust it with a little cocoa powder. Cocoa doesn't show on the baked cake like flour does.

Bake in a pre-heated 300° oven for 1 hour and 45 minutes or until a toothpick inserted near the center comes out clean. Let the cake cool almost to room temperature before inverting the pan. A slice of this cake toasted in the oven and spread with butter is almost pure heaven in the morning when accompanied by a cup of coffee or a cold glass of milk.

*The Hershey company produced the first milk chocolate bar!*

**Fig. 1.**

**Fig. 2.**

**Fig. 3.**

**Fig. 4.**

**4.** Make center squares by sewing each of three red 2½" x 42" strips to three blue/brown print strips. Cut strips into (36) 2½" segments (Fig. 2).

**5.** Sew segments together as shown in Fig. 3, making 18 center block squares.

**6.** Sew units together into strips (Fig. 4).

**7.** Sew rows together as shown in Fig. 5. Make 18 blocks.

## Quilt Top Assembly

❻ Piece six diagonal rows of blocks together with 18¼" cream triangles as indicated in Fig. 6. Sew rows together.

❻ Attach corner triangles. Press gently and trim edges of quilt as necessary.

## Borders

BORDER 1 – Sew red 2½" inner border strips together, following the instructions on page 8 for how to measure borders. Attach borders to the sides of the quilt first, then to the top and bottom.

BORDER 2 – Sew together 6½" blue/brown print border strips. Attach to either side of the quilt top, then to the top and bottom. Press borders and check for loose threads that may need to be clipped.

## Quilting and Finishing

Layer and baste the quilt top for the quilting method of your choice.

## Quilting Suggestion

For this quilt, smooth machine quilting designs were used because of the sharp points in the pieced blocks. Stippling was done on the cream background along with a very smooth feather design. Quilting in the ditch on the inner border keeps the quilt flat. Since the border print is a busy design, the quilting pattern does not show. It is a continuous line design of a flower with leaves.

Bind CHOCOLATE POUND CAKE with brown/pink binding (for directions see page 10).

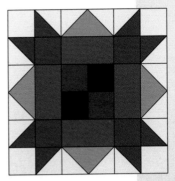

**Fig. 5.**

**Fig. 6.**

*CRÈME DE MINT, 46" x 46".*

# Crème de Mint

*We all need the gratification of a finished project, and Crème de Mint is a great quilt that goes together easily. While you are making Crème de Mint, take a short break and make some of Cathy's Thin Mint cookies, a perfect match for this fast project.*

Quilt Size: 46" x 46"
Block Size: 7½" x 7½"

## Fabric Requirements (based on 42" wide fabric)

| Fabric | Yardage | Pieces |
|---|---|---|
| Dark brown | ½ yd. | **Attic Window Blocks – Squares**<br>From 2 strips, 3" x 42"<br>cut (24) 3" squares.<br>**Attic Window Blocks – Half-square Triangles**<br>From 2 strips, 3⅜" x 42"<br>cut (24) 3⅜" squares.<br>Cut once diagonally. |
| Med. brown | ½ yd. | **Attic Window Blocks – Half-square Triangles**<br>From 1 strip, 3⅜" x 42"<br>cut (8) 3⅜" squares.<br>Cut once diagonally.<br>**Binding**<br>Cut 5 strips, 2" x 42". |
| Green plaid | ¼ yd. | **Attic Window Blocks – Squares**<br>From 2 strips, 3" x 42"<br>cut (24) 3" squares. |

**Thin Mint Cookies**
by Cathy Scovill
   12 oz. pkg. semi-sweet
      chocolate chips
   6 dozen Ritz crackers
   ¼ tsp. peppermint extract
   Creamy peanut butter

Melt chocolate chips in microwave on high for 3 minutes, or until melted. Add peppermint extract and stir until smooth.

Spread a layer of peanut butter between two crackers and dip into chocolate. Place on waxed paper to set. Makes about 3 dozen. (This is also great using graham crackers in place of Ritz crackers.)

*Thomas Gage, an English friar, reported in 1648 that chocolate was a "spicy, scummy drink" that he had tasted in the New World.*

*History of chocolate begins in 200 B.C.*

| Fabric | Yardage | Pieces |
|---|---|---|
| Green print | ⅜ yd. | **Attic Window Blocks – Half-square Triangles**<br>From 2 strips, 3⅜" x 42"<br>cut (16) 3⅜" squares.<br>Cut once diagonally. |
| | | **Monkey Wrench Blocks – Squares**<br>Cut (4) 1⅞" squares. |
| | | **Monkey Wrench Blocks – Half-square Triangles**<br>Cut (2) 2⅞" squares.<br>Cut once diagonally. |
| | | **Monkey Wrench Blocks – Half-square Triangles**<br>Cut (2) 3½" squares.<br>Cut once diagonally. |
| | | **Monkey Wrench Blocks – Half-square Triangles**<br>Cut (2) 4⅝" squares.<br>Cut once diagonally. |
| Cream print | ⅜ yd. | **Attic Window Blocks – Squares**<br>From 1 strip, 3" x 42"<br>cut (6) 3" squares. |
| | | **Monkey Wrench Blocks – Half-square Triangles**<br>Cut (4) 1⅞" squares.<br>Cut once diagonally. |
| | | **Monkey Wrench Blocks – Half-square Triangles**<br>Cut (2) 2⅞" squares.<br>Cut once diagonally. |
| | | **Monkey Wrench Blocks – Half-square Triangles**<br>Cut (2) 3½" squares.<br>Cut once diagonally. |
| | | **Monkey Wrench Blocks – Half-square Triangles**<br>Cut (2) 4⅝" squares.<br>Cut once diagonally. |
| Rust print | ⅜ yd. | **Attic Window Blocks – Squares**<br>From 1 strip, 3" x 42"<br>cut (6) 3" squares. |

| Fabric | Yardage | Pieces |
|---|---|---|
| Rust print (cont.) | | **Monkey Wrench Blocks – Half-square Triangles** |
| | | Cut (4) 1⅞" squares. |
| | | Cut once diagonally. |
| | | **Monkey Wrench Blocks – Half-square Triangles** |
| | | Cut (2) 2⅞" squares. |
| | | Cut once diagonally. |
| | | **Monkey Wrench Blocks – Half-square Triangles** |
| | | Cut (2) 3½" squares. |
| | | Cut once diagonally. |
| | | **Monkey Wrench Blocks – Half-square Triangles** |
| | | Cut (2) 4⅝" squares. |
| | | Cut once diagonally. |
| Light brown | ⅝ yd. | **Monkey Wrench Blocks – Half-square Triangles** |
| | | Cut (4) 1⅞" squares. |
| | | Cut once diagonally. |
| | | **Monkey Wrench Blocks – Half-square Triangles** |
| | | Cut (2) 2⅞" squares. |
| | | Cut once diagonally. |
| | | **Monkey Wrench Blocks – Half-square Triangles** |
| | | Cut (2) 3½" squares. |
| | | Cut once diagonally. |
| | | **Monkey Wrench Blocks – Half-square Triangles** |
| | | Cut (2) 4⅝" squares. |
| | | Cut once diagonally. |
| | | **Inner Border** |
| | | Cut 4 strips, 2½" x 42". |
| Green border | 1½ yds. | **Outer Border** |
| | | Cut 5 strips, 6½" x 42". |
| Backing | 3 yds. | |
| Cotton batting | 52" x 52" | |
| Other materials | 100% cotton thread | |
| | Rotary cutter, mat, and 6½"-wide ruler | |
| | Basic sewing supplies | |

*What is the biggest holiday for candy sales – Halloween, Easter, Valentine's Day, or Christmas? If you chose Halloween, you were correct. Halloween is the biggest candy holiday, chalking up $950 million in sales.*

*"Once in a while I say, 'Go for it,' and I eat chocolate."*
*Claudia Schiffer*

**Fig. 1.**

**Fig. 2.**

**Fig. 3.**

**Fig. 4.**

**Fig. 5.**

## Attic Window Block Assembly

**1.** With right sides together, sew the longest side of a 3⅜" medium brown half-square triangle to a 3⅜" dark brown half-square triangle (Fig. 1). Make 16 squares.

**2.** Assemble two blocks with 3" cream squares as shown in Fig. 2.

**3.** Assemble two blocks with 3" rust squares following Fig. 3.

**4.** With right sides together, sew the longest side of a 3⅜" green print half-square triangle to a 3⅜" dark brown half-square triangle (Fig. 4). Make 32 squares.

**5.** Assemble eight blocks with 3" green plaid squares (Fig. 5).

## Monkey Wrench Block Assembly

**1.** With right sides together, sew together a 1⅞" cream square and a 1⅞" green print square. Make four units. Sew two units together as shown in Fig. 6. Make two, four-patch squares.

**2.** With right sides together, sew together a 1⅞" light brown square and a 1⅞" rust square. Make four units. Sew two units together as shown in Fig. 7. Make two, four-patch squares. The cream/green squares and the light brown/rust squares are the centers of the Monkey Wrench blocks.

**3.** Referring to Fig. 8, sew 2⅞" cream and 2⅞" green print half-square triangles to cream and green four-patch squares. If necessary, trim unit to 4¼".

**4.** As shown in Fig. 9, sew 2⅞" light brown and 2⅞" rust half-square triangles to light brown and rust four-patch squares.

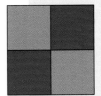
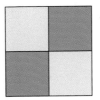

**Fig. 6.**　　　　　**Fig. 7.**

5. Sew 3½" cream and 3½" green print half-square triangles to cream and green four-patch units (Fig. 10).

6. Sew 3½" light brown and 3½" rust half-square triangles to light brown and rust four-patch units (Fig. 11).

7. Sew 4⅝" cream and 4⅝" green print half-square triangles to cream and green squares (Fig. 12, page 50) to complete two Monkey Wrench blocks.

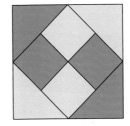

**Fig. 8.**　　　　　**Fig. 9.**

8. Sew 4⅝" light brown and 4⅝" rust half-square triangles to light brown and rust squares (Fig. 13, page 50) to complete two Monkey Wrench blocks.

## Quilt Top Assembly

❧ Connect blocks in rows of four, following the quilt assembly diagram (Fig. 14, page 50) for placement.

## Borders

BORDER 1 – Following border directions on page 8, sew light brown inner border to left and right sides of quilt.

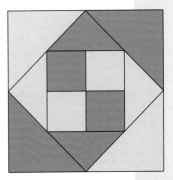

**Fig. 10.**

BORDER 2 – Sew green border strips to the left and right sides of the quilt, then to the top and bottom. Press gently.

## Quilting and Finishing

Layer and baste the quilt top for the quilting method of your choice.

## Quilting Suggestion

All the quilting for CRÈME DE MINT was done using a walking foot. Each block is quilted in the ditch. Look at the photo of the quilt and you'll see 12 dark triangles formed from the piecing. In those triangles, I quilted using a ¼" seam.

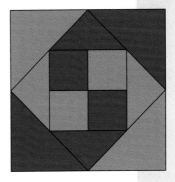

**Fig. 11.**

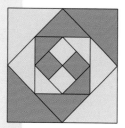

**Fig. 12.**

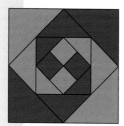

**Fig. 13.**

On this quilt or any other, remember that ¼" quilters' masking tape is not just for hand quilters. It also comes in very handy when machine quilting.

To give the quilt definition, I quilted a straight line through the center of the green plaid squares. the inner border was also quilted in the ditch. The border is simply two lines of quilting evenly spaced. This is one of my favorite quick and easy ways to quilt borders.

Bind with medium brown fabric, following directions on page 10.

**Fig. 14.**

*CHOCOLATE STIPPLED CHEESECAKE, 61" x 79".*

# Chocolate Stippled Cheesecake

There are few things on earth that compare to the decadent indulgence of eating chocolate cheesecake! Friend and fellow quilter, Cathy Scovill provided this lick-your-spoon no-bake recipe for Chocolate Stippled Cheesecake.

Mirroring the colors of the dessert, the rich browns, creamy off-whites, and golden ambers of the quilt, CHOCOLATE STIPPLED CHEESECAKE, are a feast for the eyes! This is an easy quilt to make; just be careful of the fabric placement in the blocks. And be sure to have some cheesecake on hand!

**Chocolate Stippled Cheesecake**

- 1 8 oz. pkg. cream cheese
- ¾ c. powdered sugar
- 1 8 oz. Cool Whip
  reg. or lite, no fat-free
- 1 Oreo cookie pie shell
- ½ c. semi-sweet
  chocolate chips
- ¼ tsp. peppermint extract
  (optional)

Beat together cream cheese and powdered sugar until smooth. Add Cool Whip and mix well. Spread mixture in pie shell.

Place chocolate chips in microwave and heat on high for 3 minutes or until melted. Add extract and stir until smooth. Stipple (drizzle) chocolate in a free-motion pattern over the cheesecake. Chill several hours before serving.

Quilt Size: 61" x 79"
Block: 9" x 9"

## Fabric Requirements (based on 42" wide fabric)

| Fabric | Yardage | Pieces |
|---|---|---|
| Varigated red | ⅝ yd. | **Block A – Squares**<br>From 2 strips, 3½" x 42"<br>    cut (17) 3½" squares. |
| | | **Block B – Quarter-square Triangles**<br>From 2 strips, 4¼" x 42"<br>    cut (18) 4¼" squares.<br>Cut twice diagonally. |
| Tan | 1¼ yd. | **Block A – Rectangles**<br>From 4 strips, 3½" x 42"<br>    cut (68) 2" x 3½" rectangles. |
| | | **Block A – Half-square Triangles**<br>From 1 strip, 3⅞" x 42"<br>    cut (10) 3⅞" squares.<br>Draw a diagonal line, corner<br>to corner, on wrong side. |

| Fabric | Yardage | Pieces |
|---|---|---|
| Tan (cont.) | | **Block B – Squares**<br>From 2 strips, 3½" x 42"<br>cut (24) 3½" squares.<br>**Block B – Quarter-square Triangles**<br>From 2 strips, 4¼" x 42"<br>cut (18) 4¼" squares.<br>Cut twice diagonally. |
| Navy | 1 yd. | **Block A – Rectangles**<br>From 4 strips, 3½" x 42"<br>cut (68) 2" x 3½" rectangles.<br>**Block A – Half-square Triangles**<br>From 4 strips, 3⅞" x 42"<br>cut (34) 3⅞" squares. |
| Cream | ⅞ yd. | **Block A – Half-square Triangles**<br>From 3 strips, 3⅞" x 42"<br>cut (24) 3⅞" squares.<br>Draw a diagonal line, corner<br>to corner, on wrong side.<br>**Block B – Squares**<br>From 4 strips, 3½" x 42"<br>cut (48) 3½" squares. |
| Dark red | ⅜ yd. | **Block B – Half-square Triangles**<br>From 4 strips, 3⅞" x 42"<br>cut (36) 3⅞" squares.<br>Cut once diagonally. |
| Blue print | ¼ yd. | **Block B – Quarter-square Triangles**<br>From 1 strip, 4¼" x 42"<br>cut (9) 4¼" squares.<br>Draw a diagonal line, corner<br>to corner, on wrong side. |
| Indigo print | 1¾ yd. | **Block B – Quarter-square Triangles**<br>From 1 strip, 4¼" x 42"<br>cut (9) 4¼" squares.<br>**Border 2**<br>Cut 8 strips, 6½" x 42".<br>**Binding**<br>Cut 7 strips, 2½" x 42". |
| Black/red stripe | ⅝ yd. | **Border 1**<br>Cut 7 strips, 2½" x 42". |
| Backing | 3⅞ yds. | |
| Cotton batting | 65" x 83" | |

*The first chocolate factory in what would become the United States opened in 1765 in the Massachusetts Bay Colony.*

*If your passion is truffles, you're a romantic; if you like individual candy, you are a leader...or so some people say.*

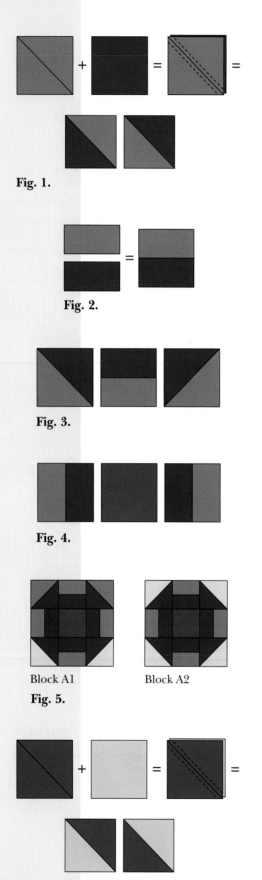

Fig. 1.

Fig. 2.

Fig. 3.

Fig. 4.

Block A1    Block A2

Fig. 5.

Fig. 6.

Other materials    100% cotton thread
Rotary cutter, mat,
and 6½"-wide ruler
Basic sewing supplies

Two basic blocks make up this quilt, but there are two color variations of Block A and three color variations of Block B. Be on your toes and make certain you have the right colors as you assemble the blocks.

## Block A Assembly

**1.** Position a 3⅞" tan square, right side up, with a 3⅞" navy square. Sew ¼" on either side of the drawn line (Fig. 1). Cut apart. Make 20 units.

**2.** Place a cream 3⅞" square with a 3⅞" navy square, right sides together and drawn side up. Sew ¼" on either side of the drawn line. Cut apart. Make 48 units.

**3.** Sew a tan 1½" x 3½" rectangle to a navy 1½" x 3½" rectangle (Fig. 2). Make 68.

**4.** Sew together two cream/navy half-square triangle units to a tan/navy rectangle unit. Make 24 units in this combination.

**5.** Sew two tan/navy half-square triangle units to a tan/navy rectangle unit (Fig. 3). Make 10.

**6.** Sew a variegated red square to two tan/navy rectangle units as shown in Fig. 4. Make 17.

**7.** Refer to Block A variations shown in Fig. 5. Make 10 of Block A1 and seven of Block A2.

## Block B Assembly

**1.** Position a 4¼" blue print square together with an indigo square of the same size, right sides together with the drawn side up. Sew ¼" on either side of the line (Fig. 6). Cut apart on the line and press open. Make 18.

**2.** Draw a diagonal line, corner to corner, on the wrong side of 9 units.

**3.** HOURGLASS UNITS – Position half-square units with right sides together and opposite fabrics facing (Fig. 7). Sew ¼" on either side of the drawn line. Cut apart and press open. Make 18 for Block B.

**4.** Sew a 4¼" quarter-square variegated red triangle to a 4¼" quarter-square tan triangle. Make 72.

**5.** As shown in Fig. 8, sew each of the 72 units to a dark red 3⅞" half-square triangle.

**6.** Make four rows for Block B1 by sewing a 3½" cream square to the above unit along with a tan 3½" square (Fig. 9).

**7.** Make 10 rows for Block B1 and B3 by sewing together tan squares and red/tan triangle units as shown in Fig. 10.

**8.** Make 16 rows for Block B2 by sewing together two cream 3½" squares to a red/tan triangle unit (Fig. 11).

**9.** Refer to the diagram of Block B variations (Fig. 12). Make four of Block B1, eight of Block B2, and six of Block B3.

## Quilt Top Assembly

☙Refer to Fig. 13, page 56, Quilt Assembly Diagram, for guidance on piecing blocks together. Sew six rows of five blocks each, paying careful attention to the placement of blocks. Stitch rows together.

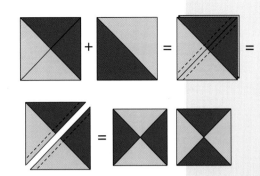

Fig. 7.

Fig. 8.

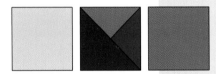

Fig. 9.

Fig. 10.

Fig. 11.

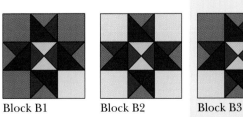

Block B1  Block B2  Block B3

Fig. 12.

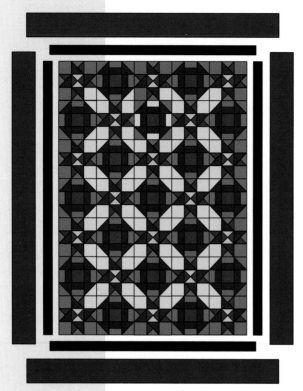

**Fig. 13.**

## Borders

BORDER 1 – Sew the 2½" strips of black/red stripe fabric together. Follow the instructions on page 8 on how to measure and sew borders. Sew black/red strips to either side, and then to the top and bottom of the quilt.

BORDER 2 – Sew together 6½" indigo print strips. Attach to either side, then to the top and bottom of the quilt. Press gently.

## Quilting and Finishing

Layer and baste quilt top for the quilting method of your choice.

## Quilting Suggestion

Wherever the tan fabric appears in the blocks, I used stippling. A free-motion design resembling four oak leaves was used in the center of each block.

Looking at the blocks, you'll notice that the sharp points really stand out in the design. Because of this, a very smooth quilting design was used in the cream areas. Actually, any feather design would look good there.

The inner border is quilted in the ditch. The outer border was quilted in a continuous line of oak leaves. A busy fabric like that used in the outer border will hide quilting mistakes, so it makes for a great opportunity to try out a design you have never used.

Bind with indigo print binding.

***BRIDGE MIX, 36½" x 44½".***

# Bridge Mix

*Are you sometimes in the mood for something but just don't know exactly what? Give* BRIDGE MIX *a try! Just like a scrap quilt, it has something for everyone. Remember to pre-wash fabrics before making your quilt.*

**Chocolate Frosting**
1 stick butter
½ c. flour
3½ T. cocoa
1 tsp. vanilla
1 box confectioners sugar
1 c. pecans, chopped

Over medium heat bring butter, cocoa, flour, and vanilla to a boil. Remove from heat, pour over confectioners sugar and stir until smooth. Add pecans and spread over brownies.

Quilt Size: 36½" x 44½"
Block: 6" x 6"

## Fabric Requirements (based on 42" wide fabric)

| Fabric | Yardage | Pieces |
|---|---|---|
| Ecru plaid | 1⅛ yds. | **Appliqué Background Squares** Cut (4) 6½" squares. **Blocks – Half-square Triangles** From 2 strips, 2⅞" x 42" cut (24) 2⅞" squares. Cut in half diagonally. |
| Lt. star print | ¼ yd. | **Blocks – Half-square Triangles** From 2 strips, 2⅞" x 42" cut (24) 2⅞" squares. Cut in half diagonally. |
| Asst. med. & dark prints | 1 yd. total | **Rows of Squares and Center Block Squares** Cut (60) 2½" squares. **Blocks – Triangles** Cut (48) 2⅞" squares. Cut in half diagonally. |

| Fabric | Yardage | Pieces |
|---|---|---|
| Orange | ½ yd. | **Appliqué Flowers** |
| | | Cut 12 Template E |
| | | **Border 1** |
| | | Cut 4 strips, 2⅞" x 42". |
| Green | ¼ yd. | **Appliqué Stems and Leaves** |
| | | Cut 8 Template A – stems |
| | | 8 Template B – straight stems |
| | | 8 Template C – sm. leaf |
| | | 8 Template D – lg. leaf |
| Brown | 1 yd. | **Border 2** |
| | | Cut 4 strips, 4½" x 42". |
| | | **Binding** |
| | | Cut 5 strips, 2½" x 42". |
| Fusible web | 1 yd. | **Appliqué Pieces** |
| | | Trace 8 Template A |
| | | 8 Template B |
| | | 8 Template C |
| | | 8 Template D |
| | | 12 Template E |
| Backing | 1½ yds. | |
| Cotton batting | 41" x 49" | |
| Other materials | 100% cotton thread | |
| | Rotary cutter, mat, and 6½"-wide ruler | |
| | Basic sewing supplies | |
| | Invisible nylon thread .004 clear | |

## Fusible Web

In the quantities listed above, trace templates A through E onto the paper side of fusible web, leaving approximately ½" between pieces.

Cut the pieces apart, leaving about ¼" around the drawn lines. Following the manufacturer's directions, fuse the pieces to wrong sides of the appropriate fabrics.

Cut the pieces out of fabrics on the drawn lines. Do not remove the paper backing until ready to fuse each piece in position.

*Some people say that if you prefer dark chocolate, you are creative!*

*Caramels are only a fad. Chocolate is a permanent thing.*
*Milton Snavely, Hershey*

**Fig. 1.**

**Fig. 2.**

**Fig. 3.**

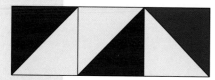

**Fig. 4.**

Fabric pieces cut from templates will be fused onto ecru plaid blocks, and then machine appliquéd along the raw edge with invisible nylon thread.

### Appliqué Assembly

❧ Finger press each of the ecru plaid 6½" squares on the diagonal in both directions (Fig. 1).

❧ Using the folds as placement guides, and looking at the picture of the quilt, layer the appliqué pieces (page 62) alphabetically. Gently fuse in place following the manufacturer's directions. Make four blocks.

❧ Machine appliqué the pieces in place using invisible nylon thread. Gently press blocks.

### Block Assembly

**1.** Sew an ecru plaid half-square triangle to a medium or dark print half-square triangle (Fig. 2). (Hint: I use four matching triangles for the star points of each block.) Make a total of 48 units, sorting by color into groups of four if desired. Press seams toward dark color.

**2.** Sew a pieced square to either side of a 2½" center block square (Fig. 3). Make 12.

**3.** Sew a light star print triangle to a medium or dark half-square triangle. Make 48 units.

**4.** Attach two of the above units to an ecru plaid half-square piece as shown in Fig. 4. Sew rows together to make 12 blocks (Fig. 5).

### Quilt Top Assembly

❧ Make four rows of (12) 2½" squares of assorted dark and medium colors.

ⓖ Referring to Fig. 6, sew center of quilt top together in rows and attach two rows of squares to top and bottom of blocks.

## Borders

BORDER 1 – Follow instructions on measuring and attaching borders on page 8. Sew 2½" strips of orange fabric to either side of the quilt, then to the top and bottom.

BORDER 2 – Sew 4½" brown print strips to either side of the quilt, then to the top and bottom. Gently press the quilt top.

## Quilting and Finishing

Layer and baste (or pin) the quilt top for the quilting method of your choice (see page 9).

## Quilting Suggestion

In BRIDGE MIX, all the appliquéd flowers, leaves, and stems were outline quilted. I stitched in the ditch the entire center of the quilt and inner border. A simple line of quilting was done in the center of the border. All quilting was done using a walking foot and invisible thread.

Bind BRIDGE MIX with brown fabric, following the directions on page 10.

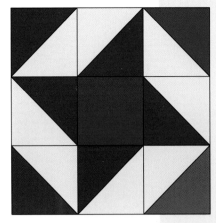

**Fig. 5.**

**Fig. 6.**

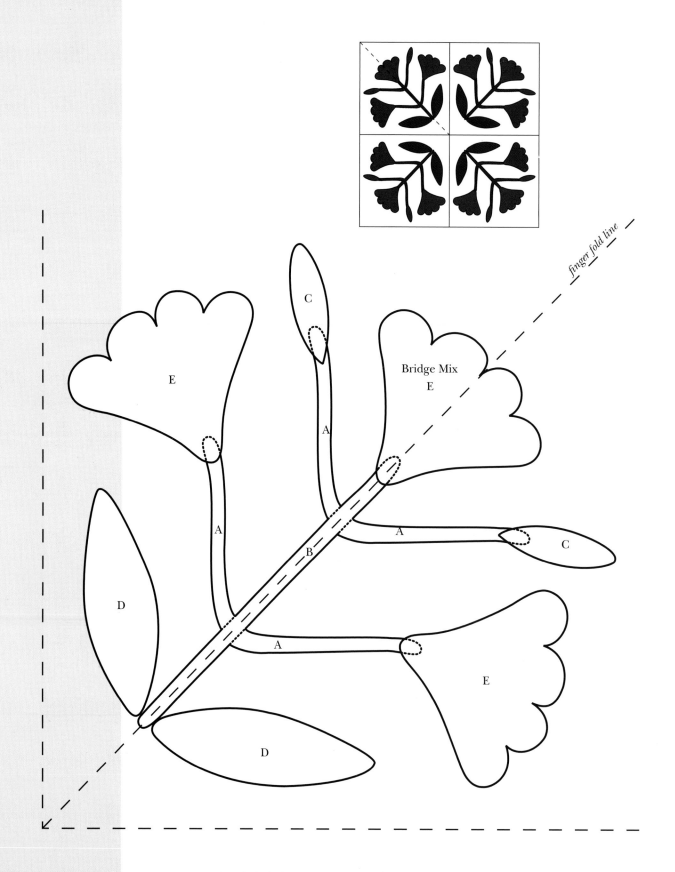

*finger fold line*

C

E

Bridge Mix
E

A

A

B

A

C

D

A

E

D

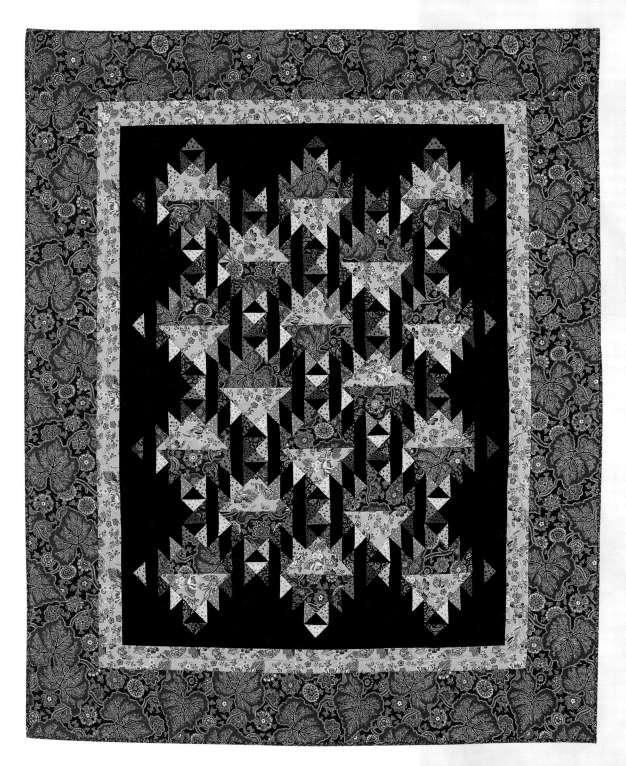

*BLACK FOREST, 50" x 60½".*

# Black Forest

At first glance, this quilt may look intimidating because of the many triangles. But it is really an easy quilt to make. You only have to cut two sizes of triangles! Using a busy fabric like the prints used here will hide any points that don't quite match. I promise you my quilt is not perfect, but I enjoy it just the same.

One tip that is very important when starting a quilt that requires a lot of cutting – put a new rotary blade in your cutter before beginning the project. You will be amazed how quickly you can cut the entire quilt.

The Black Forest No Bake Cookie recipe was born in my kitchen. A group of us declared these cookies to be the perfect inspiration for this wonderful quilt.

*The word chocolate comes from the Mayan word tchocolatl, the drink of the Mayan gods.*

Quilt Size: 50" x 60½"
Block: 7½" x 7½"

**Fabric Requirements** (based on 42" wide fabric)

| Fabric | Yardage | Pieces |
|---|---|---|
| Lg. yellow print | ¾ yd. | **Blocks – Half-square Triangles** From 2 strips, 5⅜" x 42" cut (9) 5⅜" squares. Draw a diagonal line, corner to corner, on wrong side. **Border 2** Cut 5 strips, 2½" x 42". |
| Lg. blue print | ¼ yd. | **Blocks – Half-square Triangles** From 1 strip, 5⅜" x 42" cut (5) 5⅜" squares. |

| Fabric | Yardage | Pieces |
|---|---|---|
| Red print | 2 yds. | **Blocks – Half-square Triangles** |
| | | From 1 strip, 5⅜" x 42" |
| | | cut (5) 5⅜" squares. |
| | | **Border 3** |
| | | Cut 6 strips, 6½" x 42". |
| | | **Binding** |
| | | Cut 6 strips, 2½" x 42". |
| Black tone-on-tone | 1⅜ yds. | **Blocks – Half-square Triangles** |
| | | From 9 strips, 2⅜" x 42" |
| | | cut (144) 2⅜" squares. Draw a diagonal line, corner to corner, on the wrong side with a white marker. |
| | | **Setting Triangles** |
| | | From 1 strip, 11⅞" x 42" |
| | | cut (3) 11⅞" squares. |
| | | Cut each twice on the diagonal. |
| | | **Corner Triangles** |
| | | Cut (2) 6¼" squares. |
| | | Cut once diagonally. |
| | | **Border 1** |
| | | Cut 5 strips, 1½" x 42". |
| 8 asst. fabrics | ⅛ yd. each | **Blocks – Half-square Triangles** |
| | | From each of eight fabrics cut 1 strip, 2⅜" x 42". |
| | | Cut (18) 2⅜" squares. |
| Backing | 3¼ yds. | |
| Cotton batting | 54" x 64½" | |
| Other materials | 100% cotton thread | |
| | Rotary cutter, mat, and 6½"-wide ruler | |
| | Basic sewing supplies | |

## Block Assembly

**1.** Place a large yellow print, 5⅜" square on each red print 5⅜" square and each blue print 5⅜" square with the drawn side up. Sew ¼" on either side of the drawn line (Fig. 1, page 66). Cut apart on drawn line and press open. Make a total of 9 red and yellow squares, and 9 blue and yellow squares.

**2.** With right sides together, pair a black 2⅜" square with the assorted fabric 2⅜" squares. Sew ¼" on either side of the drawn line using the same method as in Fig. 1. Cut apart on drawn line

### Black Forest No Bake Cookies

¼ c. margarine
1¼ c. sugar
½ c. milk
¼ c. cocoa
1 tsp. vanilla
1½ c. quick oats
1 c. coconut
½ c. pecans, chopped
10 oz. bottle
  maraschino cherries
1 c. mini-marshmallows

Drain liquid from cherries and cut into quarters. Pat dry with paper towels and set aside.

Mix together the margarine, sugar, milk, and cocoa in a large saucepan. Bring to a boil and boil one minute, stirring constantly.

Remove from heat and mix in vanilla, quick oats, coconut, and pecans. Gently fold in prepared cherries and marshmallows.

Drop rounded tablespoons of cookie batter onto waxed paper and allow to cool.

*Ever wonder why a chocolate chip doesn't seem to melt?*

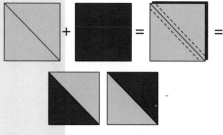

**Fig. 1.**

**Fig. 2.**

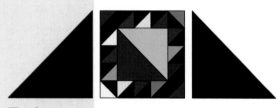

**Fig. 3.**

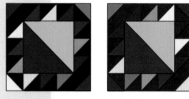

**Fig. 4.**

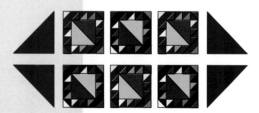

**Fig. 5.**

and press open. Make 288 half-square triangle units.

(*Author's Note:* I wanted all of my blocks to have a controlled color combination. All of the red/yellow blocks were pieced in the same color combinations in all blocks. The same was done with the blue/yellow blocks. Make one blue/yellow block and one red/yellow block first, then duplicate the same color combinations in all of the blocks.)

**3.** Referring to Fig. 2, piece nine red/yellow blocks and nine blue/yellow blocks.

## Quilt Top Assembly

As shown in Fig. 3, attach a setting triangle to either edge of a blue/yellow block.

Attach two setting triangles to a red/yellow block (Fig. 4).

While assembling the rows of blocks, turn the yellow/red blocks so the red half-square triangle is on top, and turn the blue/yellow blocks so the blue is on bottom. Sew two rows of three blocks as shown in Fig. 5. Attach setting triangles as shown.

Piece together two rows of five blocks (Fig. 6). Attach a setting triangle adjacent to a blue block on the left side of one row. Attach a setting triangle to the right side of the second row adjacent to a red block.

Sew rows together and attach corner pieces (Fig. 7). Setting triangles and corner triangles are cut large; trim quilt edges even.

**Borders** (Fig. 8)

BORDER 1 – Following instructions for measuring and attaching borders on page 8, sew the 1½" black strips to either side of the quilt, then to the top and bottom.

BORDER 2 – Attach 2½" yellow strips to either side, then to the top and bottom of the quilt.

BORDER 3 – In a similar manner, attach the 6½" red border pieces to the quilt top. Gently press the quilt.

## Quilting and Finishing

Layer and baste quilt top for the quilting method of your choice.

## Quilting Suggestion

A heart-shaped continuous line quilting design was used in the setting triangles. In all of the small block triangles, a tiny stipple makes the prints stand out. In the yellow inner border, a leaf design was quilted and in the outer border, a large meander stipple was done in red thread.

Attach red binding to the edges following the directions on page 10.

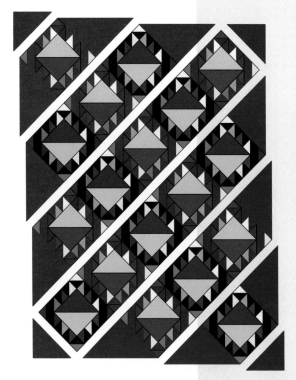

Fig. 7.

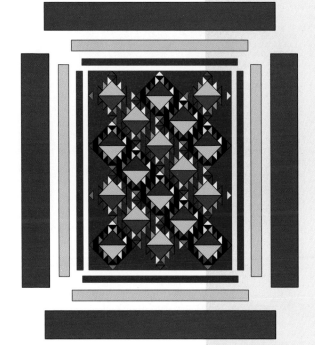

Fig. 8.

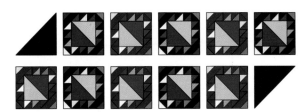

Fig. 6.

*JELLY BEANS, 50" x 50".*

# Jelly Beans

*Did you know there is a chocolate cookie flavored jelly bean? It is delicious! This quilt is made with Robert Kaufman fabrics. The fabric from which the quilt gets its inspiration is covered in jelly beans and right there beside a blueberry one is a chocolate cookie jelly bean!*

*I have not been able to decide which I enjoy most, using this quilt as a table topper, a throw, or a medallion on the guest bed. While making this quilt, see how many of the jelly bean flavors you have actually tried – you may be surprised at the variety.*

Quilt Size: 50" x 50"
Block Size: 11½" x 11½"

**Fabric Requirements** (based on 42" wide fabric)

| Fabric | Yardage | Pieces |
|---|---|---|
| 8 bright fabrics | ¼ yd. each | **Block A – Squares** |
| | | Cut (4) 3⅜" squares from each of eight fabrics. |
| | | **Block B – Squares** |
| | | Cut (5) 2½" squares from each of eight fabrics. |
| | | **Pieced Border – Half-square Triangles** |
| | | Cut (5) 2⅞" squares from each of eight fabrics. |

*By the turn of the eighteenth century, Florence and Venice were famous for their chocolate.*

*In 1579 one pirate ship burned an entire shipload of cacao beans because they believed it was sheep droppings!*

| Fabric | Yardage | Pieces |
|---|---|---|
| Red jelly bean fabric | 1⅛ yds. | **Block A – Quarter-square Triangles**<br>From 1 strip, 6" x 42"<br>  cut (8) 3¼" squares.<br>  Cut once diagonally.<br>**Corner Triangles**<br>From 1 strip, 3¼" x 42"<br>  cut (8) 3¼" squares.<br>  Cut once diagonally.<br>**Center Squares**<br>Cut (4) 3⅜" squares.<br>**Border 1**<br>Cut 4 strips, 2½" x 42".<br>**Pieced Border Corners**<br>Cut (4) 2½" squares.<br>**Outer Border Corners**<br>Cut (4) 4½" squares.<br>**Binding**<br>Cut 6 strips, 2½" x 42". |
| Off-white | 2 yds. | **Block A – Triangles**<br>From 2 strips, 3¾" x 42"<br>  cut (16) 3¾" squares.<br>  Cut once diagonally.<br>**Block B – Squares**<br>From 2 strips, 2½" x 42"<br>  cut (40) 2½" squares.<br>**Block B – Triangles**<br>From 2 strips, 6⅝" x 42"<br>  cut (10) 6⅝" squares.<br>  Cut once diagonally.<br>**Pieced Border –**<br>**Half-square Triangles**<br>From 3 strips, 2⅞" x 42"<br>  cut (40) 2⅞" squares.<br>  Draw a line, corner to<br>  corner, on wrong side.<br>**Border 3**<br>Cut 4 strips, 4½" x 42". |
| Backing | 3 yds. | |
| Cotton batting | 54" x 54" | |
| Other materials | 100% cotton thread | |
| | Rotary cutter, mat, and 6½"-wide ruler | |
| | Basic sewing supplies | |

*Be sure you have a good supply of jelly beans and let's begin!*

## Block A Assembly

**1.** Sew a quarter-square triangle of red jelly bean fabric to each side of a 3⅜" bright colored square (Fig. 1). Sew a second unit using a different colored square.

**Fig. 1.**

**2.** Sew two different 3⅜" colored squares to either side of a 3⅜" red jelly square (Fig. 2).

**Fig. 2.**

**3.** Sew segments together as shown in Fig. 3 and attach a red 3¼" half-square triangle to each corner. Trim edges even.

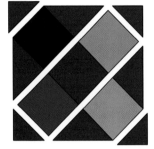
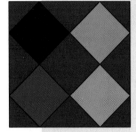

**Fig. 3.**

**4.** Referring to Fig. 4, sew an off-white half-square triangle to two sides of four, 3⅜" bright colored squares.

**5.** Attach units to the center of Block A (Fig. 5). Make four blocks following the steps above.

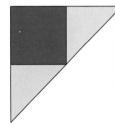

**Fig. 4.**

## Block B Assembly

**1.** Using eight different bright 2½" squares alternating with off-white 2½" squares, make the center of Block B as shown in Fig. 6, page 72.

**2.** Attach 6⅝" triangles to each side. Make five of Block B (Fig. 7, page 72).

## Quilt Top Assembly

☙ Sew three rows of three blocks each as shown in Fig. 8, page 72.

## Borders

BORDER 1 – Follow the directions on page 8 on how to measure and attach borders. Sew 2¼" red jelly bean strips to either side of the quilt, then to the top and bottom (Fig. 9, page 73).

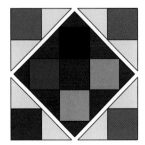

**Fig. 5.** Block A

**Fig. 6.**

**Fig. 7.** Block B

**Fig. 8.**

PIECED BORDER – With right sides together and drawn side up, place a 2⅞" square of off-white fabric together with a 2⅞" square of bright fabric. Sew ¼" on either side of the drawn line (Fig. 10). Cut apart on the drawn line. Make a total of 76 half-square triangle units.

Sew 19 triangle units into a row. Make four rows.

Attach a pieced border row to either side of the quilt with the wider part of the off-white triangles toward the center of the quilt (Fig. 11).

Sew a 2½" red jelly bean square to each end of two triangle rows (Fig. 11) and sew to the top and bottom of the quilt center.

BORDER 3 – Sew off-white border strips to either side of the quilt top. Sew a 4½" red jelly bean square to either end of two off-white border strips (Fig. 12), then attach borders to the top and bottom of the quilt.

## Quilting and Finishing

Layer and baste quilt top for the quilting method of your choice.

## Quilting Suggestion

JELLY BEANS is another quilt that I did very quickly using a walking foot. The center and inner border were stitched in-the-ditch and the border was quilted in a very easy cable design. The cable design was marked onto the quilt top with washout blue marker, then quilted with white thread.

Bind the quilt with red jelly bean fabric and make a quilt label.

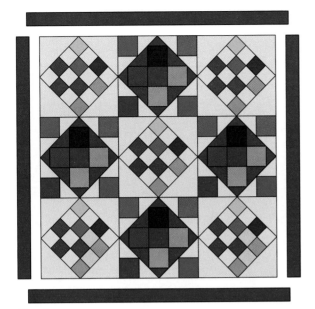

Fig. 9.

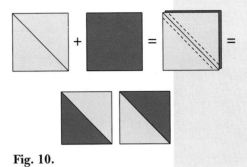

Fig. 10.

Fig. 11.

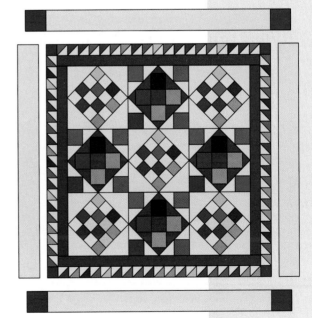

Fig. 12.

***EASTER CANDY, 44½" x 55".***

# Easter Candy

Easter Candy was designed after I saw the beautiful Benartex collection of Fossil Fern fabrics. The wonderful colors reminded me of the Easter egg hunts of my childhood, and the baskets of delicious candy. It seems everything is in pastels at Easter!

Quilt Size: 44½" x 55"
Block Size: 7½" x 7½"

## Fabric Requirements (based on 42" wide fabric)

Each of the 12 blocks in this quilt has a very light pastel background plus a dark fabric and a light fabric. Choose the color pairs you want in the centers of the blocks and place the large squares of those fabrics together. Cut 2⅜" squares for half-square triangles and 2" squares from the dark pastels.

| Fabric | Yardage | Pieces |
|---|---|---|
| Sky blue | ½ yd. | **Border 2** |
| | | Cut 5 strips, 2" x 42". |
| Yellow | ¾ yd. | **Border 3** |
| | | Cut 4 strips, 5½" x 42". |
| Very light pastel | ½ yd. | **Blocks – Squares** |
| | | From 3 strips, 2" x 42" cut (48) 2" squares. |
| | | **Blocks – Half-square Triangles** |
| | | From 4 strips, 2⅜" x 42" cut (72) 2⅜" squares. Draw a diagonal line, corner to corner on wrong side. |

*More than 60 million chocolate bunnies will be produced for Easter.*

*Speaking of chocolate bunnies, which ear do you eat first – the right or the left?*

*Chocolate is the single most craved food in the country.*

| Fabric | Yardage | Pieces |
|---|---|---|
| Rainbow | 1 yd. | **Sashing – Rectangles** |
| | | From 2 strips, 3½" x 42" |
| | | cut (17) 3½" x 8" rectangles. |
| | | **Pieced border** |
| | | From 3 strips, 2" x 42" |
| | | cut (14) 2" x 8" rectangles. |
| | | **Binding** |
| | | Cut 6 strips, 2½" x 42". |
| 12 pastels | ¼ yd. each | **Blocks – Quarter-square Triangles** |
| | | Cut (1) 5¾" square from each fabric. |
| | | **Blocks – Half-square Triangles** |
| | | Cut 1 strip, 2⅜" x 42" |
| | | from six darkest fabrics. |
| | | Cut (12) 2⅜" squares. |
| | | **Blocks – Squares** |
| | | From six darkest fabrics |
| | | cut (8) 2" squares. |
| Backing | 2⅝ yds. | |
| Cotton batting | 49" x 59" | |
| Other materials | | Sewing thread |
| | | Rotary cutter, mat, and 6½"-wide ruler |
| | | Basic sewing supplies |

See the Resources section on page 110 for information on fabrics used and kit availability.

## Block Assembly

**1.** HOURGLASS UNITS – Starting with the paired 5¾" squares (see Fabric Requirements), draw a diagonal line, corner to corner, on the wrong side of each light colored square (Fig. 1). With right sides together, sew ¼" on either side of the line. Cut apart on the line. Press open.

**2.** Place two units, right sides together, with opposing fabrics facing each other. Draw a line corner to corner on wrong side of top unit. Sew ¼" on either side of the drawn line to form an hourglass block (Fig. 2). Cut on the line and press open. Make 12 hourglass blocks.

**3.** Place a 2⅜" very light pastel square on each of (12) 2⅜" squares of various colors. Position with drawn side up and right sides together (Fig. 3). Sew ¼" on either side of the drawn line.

Cut apart on drawn line. Press open. Repeat with each of the remaining 2⅜" squares. Set aside four units of each color combination to use in sashings and pieced inner border.

**4.** Referring to Fig. 4 for piecing sequence, combine two 2⅜" half-square units and one 2" square. Make four units.

**5.** Add a very light pastel square to either end (Fig. 5). Make four units.

**6.** Complete piecing the block by assembling units as shown in Fig. 6.

**7.** Assemble 12 blocks of six color combinations.

## Quilt Top Assembly

⑥Sashing Pinwheels – Remember those four units of each color combination that we set aside earlier? Now is the time to use them. Referring to Fig. 7, page 78 sew together four units, mixing the colors. Make six pinwheel units.

⑥Sew a sashing row using three 3½" x 8" rectangles of rainbow fabric and two pinwheel units (Fig. 8, page 78).

⑥*Note:* Lay out all of your completed blocks on a design wall, bed, or floor. Arrange the blocks in four rows of three each, making sure no blocks of the same color combination are side-by-side.

⑥Sew a 3½" x 8" rainbow rectangle to the right edge of two blocks per row (Fig. 9, page 78).

⑥Referring to Fig. 10, page 78, piece together four rows of three blocks each, with a sashing strip between rows as shown.

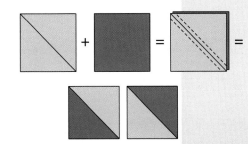

**Figs. 1.**

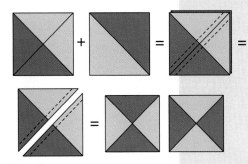

**Fig. 2.**

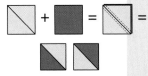

**Fig. 3.**

**Fig. 4.**

**Fig. 5.**

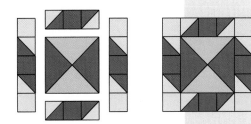

**Fig. 6.**

**Fig. 7.**

**Fig. 8.**

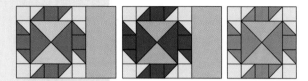

**Fig. 9.**

**Fig. 10.**

**Fig. 11.**

## Borders

PIECED INNER BORDER – Sew two 2⅜" half-square units together (Fig. 11).

Using three of the above units, three 2" x 8" rainbow rectangles, and two half-square units, sew two pieced inner border strips as shown in Fig. 12. Attach to either side of the quilt center.

Refer to Fig. 13 for assembly of top and bottom pieced inner border. Attach to quilt center.

BORDER 2 – Referring to Fig. 14, Quilt Assembly Diagram, attach 2" blue inner border strips, following instructions on page 8 for how to measure and attach borders.

BORDER 3 – Piece together yellow border strips. Attach to sides, then top and bottom of quilt. Press borders and check for loose threads that may need to be clipped.

## Quilting and Finishing

Layer and baste quilt top for the quilting method of your choice.

## Quilting Suggestion

EASTER CANDY was quilted on a long-arm sewing machine. The design is called Peacock Meander and on this quilt it is done in yellow thread. It looks just like the top of a peacock feather and the design is repeated over and over without stopping.

Bind quilt using 2½" strips of rainbow fabric.

Make a label for your quilt. How about including on the label a picture of your child dressed in Easter finery? Or maybe just a picture of a big chocolate bunny! Whatever you choose, it is sure to be special.

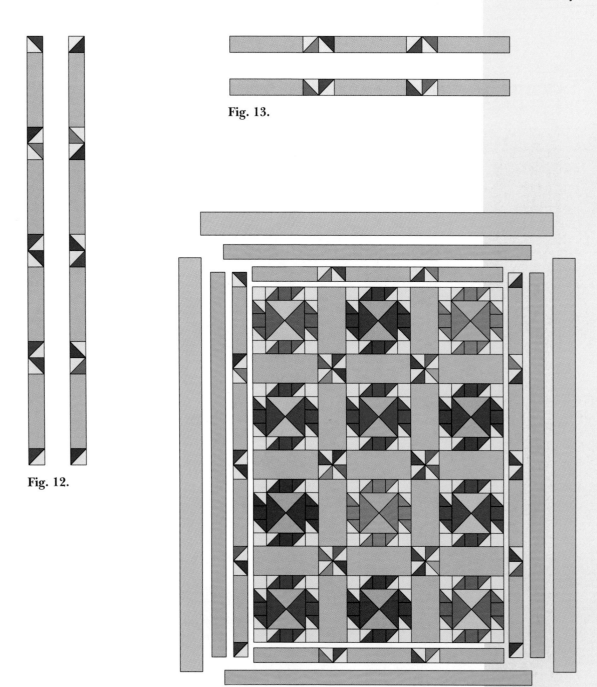

Fig. 12.

Fig. 13.

Fig. 14.

*SPRINKLES, 54" x 66".*

# Sprinkles

Once upon a time I made six dozen chocolate cupcakes for a charity bake sale. I spent hours decorating the first two dozen. Then, realizing I would never finish at that pace, I frosted the rest and topped them with colorful sprinkles. To my amazement, people couldn't wait to buy the cupcakes with sprinkles and could have cared less about the fancy decorated ones.

This quilt reminds me of the cupcakes with sprinkles and I knew this book just would not be complete without a quilt named SPRINKLES!

Quilt Size: 54" x 66"
Block Size: 12¼" x 12¼"

## Fabric Requirements (based on 42" wide fabric)

| Fabric | Yardage | Pieces |
|---|---|---|
| Eight assorted bold colors | Fat 8ths or ⅛ yd. | **Blocks – Squares** Cut (14) 2¼" squares from each fabric. |
| White | ¾ yd. | **Blocks – Half-square Triangles** From 7 strips, 2⅝" x 42" cut (108) 2⅝" squares. Cut once diagonally. |
| Gold | ½ yd. | **Border 1** Cut 5 strips, 2½" x 42". |
| Rose | 2½ yds. | **Sashings** From 12 strips, 1¾" x 42" cut (12) 1¾" x 5½" strips (12) 1¾" x 12½" strips (12) 1¾" x 17¾" strips |

*1920. The first Baby Ruth candy bar was sold. It was named for President Grover Cleveland's daughter, not the famous baseball player.*

*Chocolate candy should be mixed thoroughly into the batter or dough to protect it from direct heat during baking.*

*The melting point of cocoa butter is just below human body temperature, which is why it literally melts in your mouth, or your hand, whichever the case may be.*

| Fabric | Yardage | Pieces |
|---|---|---|
| Rose (cont.) | | **Border 2** |
| | | Cut 7 strips, 6½" x 42". |
| | | **Binding** |
| | | Cut 7 strips, 2½" x 42". |
| Pink lilac | ⅜ yd. | **Blocks – Large Triangles** |
| | | Cut (3) 12" squares. |
| | | Cut twice diagonally. |
| Wisteria | ⅜ yd. | **Blocks – Large Triangles** |
| | | Cut (3) 12" squares. |
| | | Cut twice diagonally. |
| Purple | Fat 8th or ⅛ yd. | **Blocks – Quarter-square Triangles** |
| | | Cut (3) 3¾" squares. |
| | | Cut twice diagonally. |
| Backing | 3½ yds. | |
| Cotton batting | 58" x 70" | |
| Other materials | Sewing thread | |
| | Rotary cutter, mat, and 6½"-wide ruler | |
| | Basic sewing supplies | |

This quilt is available as a kit. See the Resources section, page 110, for details.

## Block Assembly

**1.** Referring to Fig. 1, sew two white half-square triangles to each of (84) 2¼" bold-colored squares to make 84 of Unit A.

**2.** Sew two white half-square triangles to 24 bold-colored squares to make 24 of Unit B (Fig. 2).

**3.** Sew one Unit B to two Unit A's (Fig. 3) to make Unit C. Make 12 of Unit C.

**4.** Sew a Unit B to five Unit A's (Fig. 4) to make a Unit D. Make a total of 12 Unit D.

**5.** Sew a large pink lilac quarter-square triangle to a wisteria triangle of the same size. Make a total of 12 triangle units.

**6.** Referring to Fig. 5, assemble 12 blocks using the following: purple half-square triangle, 1¾" x 5½" rose strip, Unit C, 1¾" x 12½" rose strip, Unit D, 1¾" x 17¾" rose strip, pink lilac/wisteria triangle unit.

**7.** Press blocks, then trim the ends of the rose strips even with the edges of each block.

## Quilt Top Assembly

⑥ Referring to Fig. 6, page 84, piece together four rows of three blocks each in the pattern shown.

⑥ Gently press the entire quilt.

## Borders

BORDER 1 – Refer to Fig. 7, page 84, Quilt Assembly Diagram, to attach borders. Follow the instructions for measuring, piecing, and attaching borders on page 8. Attach gold 2½" border strips to either side, then to the top and bottom edges.

BORDER 2 – Sew 6½" rose border strips to the sides, then to the top and bottom of the quilt. Press again gently.

## Quilting and Finishing

Layer and baste the quilt top for the quilting method of your choice (see page 9 for basting).

## Quilting Suggestion

On this quilt, a very small stipple in white thread was used on the white background fabric. In the pink lilac/wisteria triangles, a feather design was drawn, then stitched. Stippling twice the size of that in the white background was used in the inner border. And again, stippling twice the size of that in the inner border was used in the outer border. Stitch-in-the-ditch was done along the edges of the blocks.

Bind the quilt with 2½" rose fabric following the directions on page 10.

*Anyone want a cupcake?*

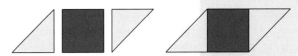
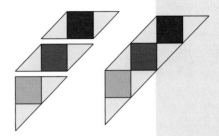

**Fig. 1.** Unit A

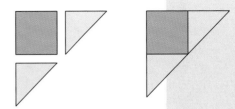

**Fig. 2.** Unit B

**Fig. 3.** Unit C

**Fig. 4.** Unit D

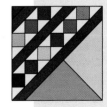

**Fig. 5.**

Fig. 6.

*Chocolate did eventually catch the attention of the Catholic Church. Its popularity in the Spanish empire raised the question of whether the rich beverage was a food, and so subject to the rules of Lent, or merely a drink. In 1569, Pope Pius V sampled a cup, but found the taste so foul that he decided there was no need to ban it.*

*America votes – chocolate is favorite flavor! 52% of Americans prefer chocolate flavor in desserts and sweet snacks.*

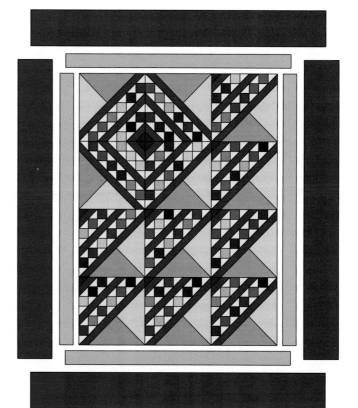

Fig. 7.

***STRAWBERRY CRÈME CENTERS, 40" x 40".***

# Strawberry Crème Centers

*Have you ever chosen a piece of candy by closing your eyes and reaching into a box of chocolates? The surprise of the center filling is part of the fun. I always seem to choose one with a rich, strawberry cream filling. So delicious!*

*That cream filling is what inspired this quilt. Next time you need inspiration, close your eyes and reach for the chocolate!*

**Double-dipped Strawberries**

Fresh strawberries with caps
Dipping chocolate bars, white
Dipping chocolate bars, dark

Wash strawberries and let dry. Place white dipping chocolate bars into a microwaveable container. The container should be small enough to give the chocolate adequate depth for dipping the berries.

Microwave on high for 45 seconds and stir; continue melting the chocolate and stirring every 30 seconds until all chocolate is melted.

Hold the berries by the cap and dip into the white chocolate leaving ¼ of the strawberry showing. Place on waxed paper.

*(continued on page 87)*

Quilt Size: 40" x 40"
Block Size: 4" x 4"

## Fabric Requirements (based on 42" wide fabric)

| Fabric | Yardage | Pieces |
|---|---|---|
| Dark pink | ⅜ yd. | **Blocks – Half-square Triangles**<br>From 2 strips, 4⅞" x 42"<br>cut (16) 4⅞" squares.<br>**Center Appliqué**<br>Cut 1 Template B. |
| Lt. pink dots | ½ yd. | **Blocks – Half-square Triangles**<br>From 2 strips, 4⅞" x 42"<br>cut (16) 4⅞" squares.<br>Draw a line, corner to corner on wrong side of fabric.<br>**Center Squares**<br>Cut (4) 4½" squares. |

| Fabric | Yardage | Pieces |
|---|---|---|
| Pink/white floral | 1⅝ yds. | **Blocks – Half-square Triangles**<br>From 4 strips, 2⅞" x 42"<br>    cut (56) 2⅞" squares.<br>    Draw a line, corner to corner,<br>    on wrong side of fabric.<br>**Outer Block – Triangles**<br>Cut 5 strips, 2⅝" x 42".<br>    Cut 40 triangles, 2⅝" x 5¼"<br>    using Omnigrid™ ruler (Fig.1).<br>**Binding**<br>Cut 4 strips, 2½" x 42". |
| Yellow dot | ¼ yd. | **Blocks – Half-square Triangles**<br>From 1 strip, 2⅞" x 42"<br>    cut (14) 2⅞" squares.<br>    Draw a line, corner to corner,<br>    on wrong side of fabric.<br>**Appliqué Pieces**<br>Cut (3) Template A |
| Lt. green floral | ¼ yd. | **Blocks – Half-square Triangles**<br>From 1 strip, 2⅞" x 42"<br>    cut (14) 2⅞" squares.<br>    Draw a line, corner to corner,<br>    on wrong side of fabric.<br>**Appliqué Pieces**<br>Cut 3 Template A |
| Dk. green floral | ¼ yd. | **Blocks – Half-square Triangles**<br>From 1 strip, 2⅞" x 42"<br>    cut (14) 2⅞" squares.<br>    Draw a line, corner to corner,<br>    on wrong side of fabric.<br>**Appliqué Pieces**<br>Cut 3 Template A |
| Pink floral | ¼ yd. | **Blocks – Half-square Triangles**<br>From 1 strip, 2⅞" x 42"<br>    cut (14) 2⅞" squares.<br>    Draw a line, corner to corner,<br>    on wrong side of fabric.<br>**Appliqué Pieces**<br>Cut 3 Template A |

When the white chocolate is set, repeat the melting process with the dark chocolate dipping bars. When dipping into dark chocolate leave approximately ¼" of the white chocolate showing. Place on waxed paper. Ready to eat as soon as the chocolate is set.

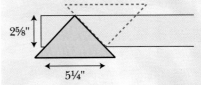

**Fig. 1.**

*71% of American chocolate eaters prefer milk chocolate.*

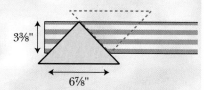

3⅜"

6⅞"

**Fig. 2.**

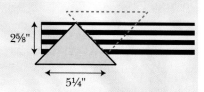

2⅝"

5¼"

**Fig. 3.**

*In 1868 Richard Cadbury introduced the first Valentine's Day box of chocolates.*

*About 65% of American candy brands have been around for more than 50 years.*

| Fabric | Yardage | Pieces |
|---|---|---|
| Dk. pink stripe | ¾ yd. | **Outer Block – Triangles**<br>From 6 strips, 3⅜" x 24"<br>(lengthwise grain of fabric)<br>cut (36) 3⅜" x 6⅞" triangles<br>using Omnigrid™ triangle ruler<br>(Fig. 2). |
| Blk/white stripe | ½ yd. | **Outer Block – Triangles**<br>From 5 strips, 2⅝" x 24"<br>(lengthwise grain of fabric)<br>cut (32) 2⅝" x 5¼" triangles<br>using Omnigrid™ triangle ruler<br>(Fig. 3). |
| Fusible web | ¼ yd. | **Appliqué Pieces**<br>Cut 8 Template A<br>1 Template B |
| Backing | 1¾ yds. | |
| Cotton batting | 43" x 43" | |
| Other materials | | Omnigrid™ triangle shaped ruler #98L<br>Rotary cutter, mat, and 6½"-wide ruler<br>Cotton thread<br>Pink thread for stitching appliqué<br>Basic sewing supplies |

## Fusible Web

In the quantities listed above, trace Templates A and B onto the paper side of fusible web, leaving ½" between pieces.

Cut the pieces apart, leaving about ¼" around the drawn lines. Following the manufacturer's directions, fuse the pieces to the wrong sides of the appropriate fabrics.

Cut the pieces out of fabrics on the drawn lines. Do not remove the paper backing until ready to fuse each piece in position.

## Block Assembly

**1.** With right sides together, place each 4⅞" square of light pink dots on a 4⅞" dark pink square, with the drawn side up. Sew ¼" on either side of the drawn line (Fig. 4). Cut apart on drawn line and press open. Make 32 half-square units.

**2.** With right sides together, pair a 2⅞" square of pink and white floral together with one 2⅞" square of yellow dot, light green floral, dark green floral, and pink floral. Using the same method as shown in Fig. 4, with drawn side up, sew ¼" on either side of the line. Cut apart on the drawn line and press open. Make 112 squares.

**3.** Sew together four squares to make a block (Fig. 5). Make 28 blocks, always placing the fabrics in the same position in each block.

**4.** Following the manufacturer's directions, fuse three Template A pieces to each 4½" square of light pink dots (Fig. 6). Buttonhole stitch around Template A pieces by hand or machine.

**5.** Sew two center squares together as shown in Fig. 7. Make two such units.

## Quilt Top Assembly

❦ Referring to Fig. 8, page 90, and paying careful attention to block rotation, sew together eight rows of eight blocks as shown.

❦ Following the manufacturer's directions for fusible web, fuse a Template B piece to the center of Templates A. Buttonhole stitch around Template B.

## Pieced Border Assembly

❦ Sew 32 black and white striped triangles to 32 pink and white floral triangles in pattern shown in Fig. 9, page 90.

❦ Sew each of the pink and white floral/black and white striped triangle units to a pink stripe triangle (Fig. 10, page 90). Make 32 blocks.

❦ Sew triangle blocks into four rows of eight blocks each. Pay careful attention to the rotation of the blocks (Fig. 11, page 90).

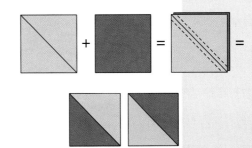

**Fig. 4.**

**Fig. 5.**

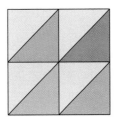

**Fig. 6.**

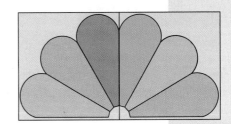

**Fig. 7.**

**Fig. 8.**

**Fig. 9.**

**Fig. 10.**

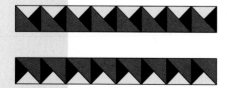

**Fig. 11.**

❻ Sew two light pink triangles together for corner blocks (Fig. 12). Make four. Attach each unit to a pink stripe triangle to make four corner blocks.

❻ Attach corner blocks to either end of two rows (Fig. 13).

❻ Attach a row of eight blocks without corner blocks to either side of the quilt top as shown in Fig. 14, Quilt Assembly Diagram.

❻ Attach the two rows with corner pieces to the top and bottom of the quilt (Fig. 14).

❻ Layer and baste for the quilting method of your choice.

**Quilting Suggestion**

This quilt was quilted quickly and easily with in-the-ditch stitches using invisible thread. Every seam has a high and a low side caused by pressing the seam allowances one way or the other. To stitch in the ditch, simply sew on the side without seam allowances.

When preparing for machine quilting, thread selection is a very important decision. For invisible thread, choose either clear or smoke in a .004 thickness. As a rule, cheaper is not better when selecting thread.

Bind quilt with light pink print binding, following the instructions on page 10.

**Fig. 12.**

**Fig. 13.**

SCC

Template
B

**Fig. 14.**

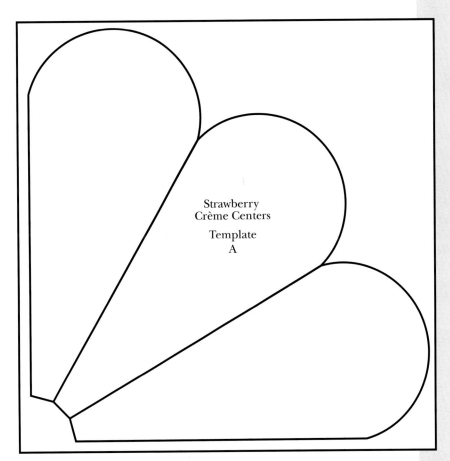

Strawberry
Crème Centers

Template
A

Template and placement guide.

***BLUEBERRIES & WHITE CHOCOLATE, 58½" x 58½".***

# Blueberries & White Chocolate

*This quilt has many techniques but all are fairly easy. The appliqué flowers are done with fusible web. The flower centers have beautiful French knots made with metallic threads. If you have always wanted to do a classic blue and white quilt, I think you will really enjoy doing this one.*

Quilt Size: 58½" x 58½"
Block Size: 10½" x 10½"
Paper Pieced Block Size: 3½" x 3½"

**Fabric Requirements** (based on 42" wide fabric)

| Fabric | Yardage | Pieces |
|---|---|---|
| Blue/white print | 1¼ yds. | **Blocks – Hourglass Quarter Squares** |
| | | From 2 strips, 4¾" x 42" |
| | | cut (12) 4¾" squares. |
| | | Draw a line, corner to corner, |
| | | on wrong side. |
| | | **Squares** |
| | | From 5 strips, 4" x 42" |
| | | cut (48) 4" squares. |
| | | **Paper Pieced Squares** |
| | | Use scraps to form background |
| | | of center blocks. |
| White tone-on-tone | 2½ yds. | **Border 2** |
| | | (Cut on lengthwise grain of fabric.) |
| | | Cut 4 strips, 6½" x LOF. |

*What is white chocolate? Real white chocolate is mainly cocoa butter, sugar, milk, and vanilla. If the ingredients say, "made with vegetable oils," it is an imitation!*

*Women prefer chocolate more than men do. A total of 57% women said chocolate was their favorite flavor compared to 46% of men.*

*Did you know cocoa beans were used as "coins" by the Aztecs?*

| Fabric | Yardage | Pieces |
|---|---|---|
| White tone-on-tone (cont.) | | **Center Square**<br>Cut (1) 12½" square.<br>**Setting Triangles**<br>Cut (2) 16⅛" squares.<br>  Cut once diagonally.<br>**Corner Triangles**<br>Cut (2) 8⅜" squares.<br>  Cut once diagonally. |
| Dark blue | 22" sq. | **Bias Stems**<br>Cut 2 bias strips, 1" x 26" &<br>  2 bias strips, 1" x 17" |
| Med. blue | ¼ yd. | **Appliqué Leaves**<br>Cut 20 Template B. |
| 10 asst. blues | 2½ yds.<br>total | **Appliqué Petals**<br>Cut 144 Template A.<br>**Border 1**<br>Cut 1 strip, 1½" x 42",<br>  from eight fabrics.<br>**Blocks – Hourglass Quarter Squares**<br>Cut (36) 4¾" squares.<br>  Draw a line corner to corner,<br>  on the wrong side.<br>**Paper Pieced Squares**<br>Use scraps to make star triangles<br>  for center blocks.<br>**Binding**<br>Cut 1 strip, 2½" x 42"<br>  from eight fabrics. |
| Fusible web | 1 pkg. | Trace 144 Template A.<br>Trace 20 Template B. |
| Backing | 3¾ yds. | |
| Cotton batting | 63" x 63" | |
| Other materials | 4 spools very fine dark blue metallic thread<br>(for machine or hand stitch in flowers)<br>#16 royal blue metallic braid medium<br>⅛" blue metallic ribbon<br>¹⁄₁₆" medium blue metallic ribbon<br>⅛" silver metallic ribbon<br>¹⁄₁₆" ice blue metallic ribbon<br>¼" metal bias bars |

Smoke-colored invisible thread .004m
Large eye needle for making French knots
Water soluble fabric glue
Rotary cutter, mat, and 6½"-wide ruler
Ordinary kitchen freezer paper
100% cotton sewing thread
Various blue threads to match fabric of petals, leaves, and vines
Basic sewing supplies

See the Resources section, page 110, for information on obtaining this quilt as a kit and for the specific fabrics and materials used in this quilt.

## Fusible Web

In the quantities listed above, trace templates A and B onto the paper side of fusible web, leaving approximately ½" between pieces.

Cut the pieces apart, leaving about ¼" around the drawn line. Following the manufacturer's directions, fuse the pieces to the wrong sides of the appropriate fabrics.

Cut the pieces out of the fabrics on the drawn lines. Do not remove the paper backing until ready to fuse each piece in position.

## Center Block Squares

1. Make 12 copies of the paper piecing pattern (page 102) for the 3½" center block squares. Add seam allowances by eye while cutting fabric for each piece. Make 12 paper pieced blocks following the directions for paper piecing shown on page 97.

The paper piecing pattern for the center squares is divided into four sections. After piecing, connect the sections to form a 3½" finished square.

(Here's a helpful tip: On my paper patterns, I write "Dk-B" in the sections needing dark blues and "L-B" in those sections needing light blues. I'm all for the small things that make life easier.)

Refer to the quilt photo for color guidance when piecing the squares.

*Use care when melting chocolate chips or pieces. Though they will appear formed after heating, they will become fluid after stirring.*

*Did you know chocolate and truffles are top choices as aphrodisiacs.*

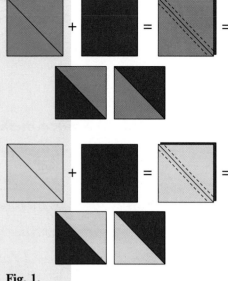

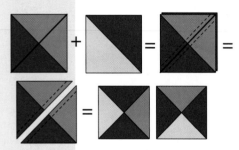

**Fig. 1.**

**Fig. 2.**

**Fig. 3.**

**Fig. 4.**

## Large Star Block Assembly

**1.** Pair together a 4¾" square of blue/white print with a 4¾" square of the assorted blues. With right sides together and the drawn side up, sew ¼" on either side of the drawn line (Fig. 1). Cut apart on drawn line and gently press open. Make 24 units.

**2.** With right sides together, pair a 4¾" square of assorted blue with another assorted blue, drawn side up. Follow procedure in Fig. 1 to make 24 half-square triangle units.

**3.** Draw a diagonal line on the wrong side of light blue half-square triangle units. Pair each with a half-square triangle unit of assorted blue triangles, with right sides together and the drawn side up (Fig. 2). Rotate the squares so lights face darks and darks face lights. Sew ¼" on either side of the drawn line. Cut apart and gently press open. Make 48 units.

**4.** Refer to Fig. 3 to piece rows together for star blocks. For each block, use blue/white print 4" squares, quarter-square triangle units, and a paper pieced center block as shown. (Paper piecing patterns found on page 102.) Make 12 blocks.

## Center Appliqué Square

**1.** Finger crease the 12½" center square twice from corner to corner. The fold lines will serve as placement guides for the appliqué design.

**2.** Following the manufacturer's directions for fusible web, fuse 12 Template A flower petals in each of four sections of the center square as shown in Fig. 4. Buttonhole stitch the petals in place.

**3.** Trim appliquéd block to 11".

# *Paper Piecing*

Paper piecing patterns can be copied using a copy machine but beware, photocopiers tend to distort patterns. If you are having copies made at a retail copy center be sure to tell the clerk that they need to be exact. Many of the really good machines at copy centers are accurate.

Please, because of copyright restrictions, copy patterns only for your own use and do not share them with others. Of course you can also trace the patterns yourself. When tracing patterns, I always use very, very, inexpensive paper since each paper pattern is used just once and then is torn away from the fabric.

In paper piecing, fabric pieces are sewn directly onto the printed (or traced) lines of the paper. Since paper dulls needles, after you're done paper piecing remember to change your sewing machine needle before doing regular sewing.

For paper piecing, make your machine stitches much smaller than normal — about 18 per inch.

**General supplies for paper piecing**

> Sewing machine
> Paper scissors
> Iron and ironing board
> Straight pins
> Glue stick (optional)

Each fabric piece needs to be just large enough to cover the patch on the paper with a ¼" seam allowance on all sides. To make sure a scrap is large enough, place it behind the pattern and hold both up to the light. Remember, larger is better!

❻ Trim each paper pattern to about ½" beyond the outside of the block but do not cut the inner pieces apart. Fabric pieces are sewn together onto the paper pattern in numerical order.

❻ To begin, place the fabric piece you want in the Number 1 section, right side up, on the unprinted side of the pattern. Hold the pattern and fabric to the light to adjust the position of the fabric. Then use a dab of glue or a straight pin to hold that piece in place.

❻ Now you are ready for fabric piece Number 2. Place it on top of piece Number 1 with right sides together, again making sure that fabric piece Number 2 is larger than the patch outline by at least ¼". Pin Number 2 in place. Turn the pattern over so the printed side is facing toward you. Start sewing on the line between piece Number 1 and Number 2. Make three or four stitches before the line begins and after the line ends. Do not back-stitch. Turn the pattern again and gently press the seam open. Never tear off the paper until the entire pattern is completed. Trim your pieced seam allowances to ¼".

❻ Choose the Number 3 fabric and place it on top of piece Number 2 with right sides together. Hold the pieces securely in place as you turn over the pattern. Again, sew with the printed side of the pattern facing you, sewing on the line between Number 2 and Number 3. Trim the seam allowance and gently press the pieces open. Repeat the directions above until all the pieces are stitched.

The paper pieced squares in BLUEBERRIES AND WHITE CHOCOLATE are constructed in four units. First sew the units and then stitch them together leaving the paper on! Or, if you prefer, you can trim the paper away from the outside seam allowances before sewing the units together. That's all there is to it. Pretty easy, huh?

**Fig. 5.**

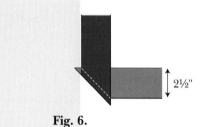

2½"

**Fig. 6.**

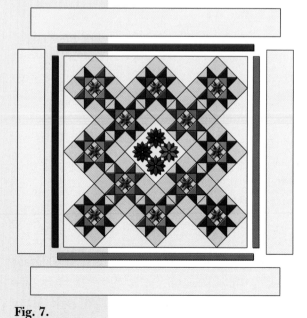

**Fig. 7.**

## Quilt Top Assembly

⑥ Assemble five rows of blocks with setting triangles as shown in Fig. 5.

⑥ Attach corner triangles. Press gently and trim edges of quilt even.

## Border 1

Sew 1½" strips of blue fabric together to make inner border (Fig. 6).

Following the instructions on page 8 for how to measure and sew borders, attach blue border to the right and left sides of the quilt, then to the top and bottom (Fig. 7).

## Border 2

Attach white tone-on-tone 6½" border strips to either side, then to the top and bottom of the quilt.

## Border appliqué

Fold bias strips in half lengthwise with wrong sides together. Stitch an accurate ¼" seam allowance from the **folded** edge. (No, that is not a typo!) Measure seam allowances from the folded side instead of the usual method of stitching from raw edges.

After sewing approximately 6 inches, remove the strip from the machine and insert a ¼" metal bias bar into the fabric tube to check for accuracy. The bias bar should fit very snugly inside the fabric tube. If it is a snug fit, remove the bias bar and continue sewing. Stitch all bias tubes in a similar manner.

Insert a metal bias bar into a fabric tube and trim the seam allowance to about ⅛". Move the seam allowance to the center of the bar and press, using steam. To assure a flat and creased bias tube, let the bar cool before removing the bias bar.

Referring to the quilt photo for placement, attach bias stem pieces to the upper left and lower right corners of the quilt. Using a very small amount of glue to hold the stems in place makes stitching much easier.

For those who need more help than simply looking at a photo for placement, here's another suggestion that might help.

Cut two strips of ordinary kitchen freezer paper the exact length and width of your top and side borders. Tape the two together at right angles (Fig. 8).

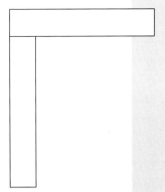

**Fig. 8.**

Fold the paper at the corner (Fig. 9), forming a miter that represents the corner of your quilt. Then draw your line or stem curves onto one thickness of the freezer paper (Fig. 10). With the paper still folded, cut on the drawn line. Separate the cut pieces and discard the outside piece.

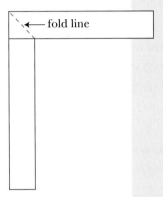

**Fig. 9.**

Open the inside pattern piece and align it with the border seam on the quilt top. Using the freezer paper as a template, draw the stem placement onto your quilt border with the fabric marker of your choice (Fig. 11). Turn the template upside down to mark stems on the opposite corner.

Machine or hand stitch bias stems in place.

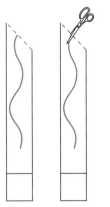

**Fig. 10.**

Referring to the photo for placement, fuse four 12-petal flowers to the borders on top of the stem pieces.

## Appliqué Finishing

Sew metallic veins in the centers of all flowers and leaves. This can be done by hand or by machine (see Couching section page 100). Use metallic thread for the top thread

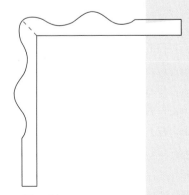

**Fig. 11.**

# Couching *or*
## Using Special Threads in the Bobbin Case

The fancy threads used to decorate the flowers in BLUEBERRIES & WHITE CHOCOLATE were threaded through the top of my machine. For those of you who may encounter problems, this section will explain how to use the thread in your bobbin case. This is called couching and it requires sewing from the wrong side of your quilt.

To use most novelty threads means having to adjust the tension of the bobbin case. The tension of the bobbin case I use every day is perfect so I always use a different one for special threads. To wind a bobbin, place the bobbin on the machine without threading the tension assembly or the guides. Your fingers will do the job of holding the thread taut as the machine slowly does the turning while the bobbin fills. Place the filled bobbin in the case and adjust the tension until it feels similar to when you are using regular thread. When couching, I always use nylon thread for the top thread. To secure the threads, the simplest method is to make three or four very short straight stitches.

# French Knots

To make French knots, bring your needle up through the center of each flower and wrap the thread around the needle three to four times. Hold the thread firmly and push the needle back down through the flower as close as possible to where it first came out (Fig. 12).

and invisible thread in the bobbin of your sewing machine (see the Resources section, page 110, for the author's thread preferences). Loosen the top tension slightly and stitch the veins using free motion stitches.

### French Knots

Make French knots in the centers of all flowers using the braid and ribbons shown in the materials list. (See French Knots, left, for instructions.)

### Quilting and Finishing

Layer and baste quilt top for the quilting method of your choice.

### Quilting Suggestion

Once again smooth quilting designs were used because of the sharp points in the piecing and appliqué. In the border, a free-form echo quilting was used. In keeping with the soft lines of the quilting, a feather design was also used.

All the star blocks were stitched in the ditch and a stipple was used on all areas with the blue and white print.

Piece binding strips together using same method as shown in Fig. 6, page 98. Attach to edges of quilt following instructions on page 10.

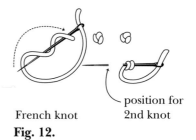

French knot     position for 2nd knot

**Fig. 12.**

Blueberries &
White Chocolate

Template A

flower

Blueberries &
White Chocolate

Template B

leaf

*finger fold line*

Placement guide

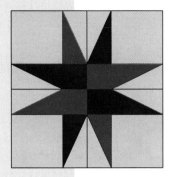

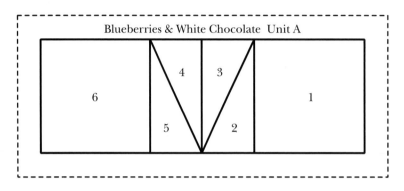

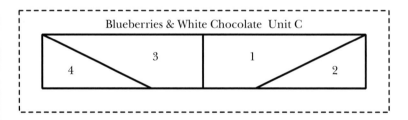

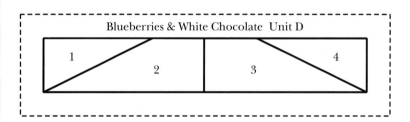

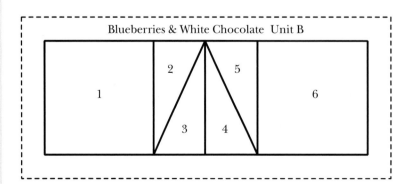

***MY HEART BELONGS TO CHOCOLATE, 52" x 52".***

# My Heart Belongs to Chocolate

*When you think of Valentine's Day, what do you think of first? Why chocolate of course! This is a great quilt for any time of year but let me warn you, have plenty of chocolate on hand. This quilt looks good enough to eat.*

*The recipe, My Heart to Your Hips Delight, is way beyond good enough to eat — it's to die for! Lucy Fazely, who pieced the quilt top, also contributed the recipe for this brownie-like dessert.*

**My Heart to Your Hips Delight**

Preheat oven to 350 degrees. Grease a springform pan (can also be made in an 8" x 12" pan).

1¼ c. butter or margarine
¾ c. baking cocoa
2 c. sugar
4 eggs, beaten
1 tsp. vanilla
1¼ c. flour
½ tsp. salt
2 c. finely chopped walnuts
6 oz. mini-chocolate chips

Over low heat, melt butter and mix in cocoa. Add sugar and stir until shiny. Remove from heat, mix in eggs and vanilla. Stir in flour, salt, and walnuts.

*(continued on page 105)*

Quilt Size: 52" x 52"
Block Size: 12" x 12"

**Fabric Requirements** (based on 42" wide fabric)

| Fabric | Yardage | Pieces |
| --- | --- | --- |
| Asst. red prints | 1 yd. total | **Blocks – Half-square Triangles** From assorted red fabrics cut (80) 3⅞" squares. |
| Asst. lt. prints | 1 yd. total | **Blocks – Half-square Triangles** From assorted light prints cut (72) 3⅞" squares. Draw a line, from corner to corner, on the wrong side. |
| Lt. beige print | 1½ yds. | **Outer Border** Cut 4 strips, 3½" x 42". **Corner Blocks** From 2 strips, 3½" x 42" cut (16) 3½" squares. |

| Fabric | Yardage | Pieces |
|---|---|---|
| Lt. beige print (cont.) | | **Inner Border** |
| | | **Half-square Triangles** |
| | | From 1 strip, 3⅞" x 42" |
| | | cut (8) 3⅞" squares. |
| | | Draw a line, corner to corner, |
| | | on the wrong side. |
| | | **Inner Border – Rectangles** |
| | | From 3 strips, 3½" x 42" |
| | | cut (4) 3½" x 6½" rectangles |
| | | (8) 3½" x 9½" rectangles. |
| | | **Corner Blocks – Squares** |
| | | Cut (4) 2½" squares. |
| | | **Appliqué Hearts** |
| | | Cut 12 Template A |
| Dk. red print | 1½ yds. | **Corner Blocks – Rectangles** |
| | | From 1 strip, 3½" x 42" |
| | | cut (16) 2½" x 3½" rectangles |
| | | **Inner Border** |
| | | Cut 5 strips, 2½" x 42". |
| | | **Appliqué Hearts** |
| | | Cut 9 Template A |
| | | **Binding** |
| | | Cut 6 strips, 2½" x 42". |
| Fusible web | 1 yd. | **Appliqué Hearts** |
| | | Cut 21 Template A |
| White braid ⅛ metallic | 6 yds. | **Hearts Embellishment** |
| | | Cut (9) 24" pieces |
| Chocolate braid ⅛ metallic | 8 yds. | **Hearts Embellishment** |
| | | Cut (12) 24" pieces |
| Backing | 3⅓ yds. | |
| Cotton batting | 56" x 56" | |
| Other materials | 100% cotton thread | |
| | Rotary cutter, mat, and 6½"-wide ruler | |
| | Large-eye needle | |
| | Basic sewing supplies | |

See the Resources section on page 110 for fabrics, kit availability, and for thread used.

## Fusible Web

Trace 21 Template A hearts onto the paper side of fusible web, leaving approximately ½" between pieces.

Pour into springform pan and bake about 40 minutes (25 minutes for an 8" x 12" pan), or until done.

Frost as soon as it comes out of the oven.

**Chocolate Frosting**
(double for recipe baked in an 8" x 12" pan)
½ stick margarine
2 T. baking cocoa
3 T. milk
2 c. powdered sugar
½ tsp. vanilla
¼ c. finely chopped walnuts

Combine margarine, cocoa, and milk in a saucepan. Bring to a boil, stirring constantly.

Remove from heat and add sugar and vanilla. Pour frosting mixture on top of baked dessert as soon as it comes out of the oven. The frosting will harden quickly, so sprinkle immediately with finely chopped walnuts.

Allow to cool. Cut into wedges like a cheesecake for serving.

*More than 35 million heart-shaped boxes of chocolate are sold for Valentine's Day.*

*Though a cacao tree
(chocolate tree)
can bear fruit for
40 years, a lifetime's
yield of beans may
equal no more than
200 pounds!*

*When melting solid
chocolate in a
microwave oven, it is
best to melt only small
amounts at a time.
Milk chocolate tends
to scorch easily.*

Cut the pieces apart, leaving about ¼" around the drawn lines. Following the manufacturer's directions, fuse the pieces to the wrong sides of the light beige print and dark red print.

Cut apart on the drawn lines. Do not remove the paper backing until ready to fuse each piece in position.

**Block Assembly**

1. With right sides together, place a 3⅞" light print square with a 3⅞" red print square. With drawn side up, sew ¼" on either side of the diagonal line (Fig. 1). Cut apart on drawn line as shown and press open. Make 144.

2. Position a 3⅞" light beige print square on each of eight 3⅞" red print squares. Sew ¼" on either side of the diagonal line. Cut apart on drawn line and press open. Set these units aside for use in the border.

3. Arrange the pieced half-square triangle units to make a block as shown in Fig. 2. Make nine blocks.

**Quilt Top Assembly**

❺ Sew blocks together in three rows of three each (Fig. 3).

❺ Sew rows together to form the quilt center (Fig. 4, page 108). Press gently.

**Borders**

Sew together two 3½" x 9½" rectangles, two red print and light beige print half-square units, and one 3½" x 6½" rectangle (Fig. 5, page 108) to form pieced inner border strips. Make four.

Sew a 3½" light beige strip to a 2½" dark red print strip (Fig. 6, page 108). Make four. Trim all four border strip sets the same length as the pieced border strips.

Sew a pieced border to a light beige and dark red print border unit (Fig. 7, page 108). Make four.

Corner blocks – Using four 3½" light beige squares, four 2½" x 3½" dark red print rectangles, and one 2½" light beige print square, assemble corner blocks as shown in Fig. 8, page 108.

As shown in Fig. 9, page 109, Quilt Assembly Diagram, attach a border unit to either side of the quilt center.

Sew corner blocks to either end of two border units as shown in Fig. 9, page 109. Attach to top and bottom of quilt. Press quilt top.

## Appliqué

⑥ Position light hearts on dark diamonds and dark hearts on light diamonds, following the placement diagram (Fig. 10, page 109).

⑥ Following the manufacturer's directions for fusible web, fuse the hearts in position on the quilt top (Fig. 11, page 109).

⑥ Buttonhole stitch around each heart.

⑥ Apply "chocolate drizzle" braid to the appliqué hearts using a very narrow zig-zag stitch (1.0 width with .75 length) and .004mm invisible nylon thread. Use white braid on dark hearts and brown braid on light hearts. Leave 6" to 8" of loose braid at the beginning and ending.

⑥ Note: To secure the invisible thread at the beginning and end, turn the stitch width to near 0 and make six stitches in the background as close as possible to the appliqué piece.

## Quilting and Finishing

Gently press the entire quilt top; layer and baste for the quilting method of your choice.

Thread a large eye needle with the loose braid around the hearts. Bury the braid in the batting.

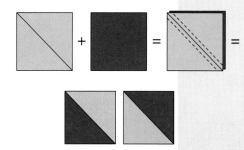

Fig. 1.

Fig. 2.

Fig. 3.

**Fig. 4.**

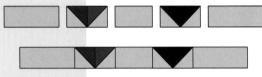

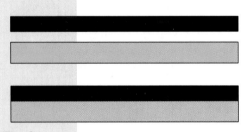

**Fig. 5.**

**Fig. 6.**

**Fig. 7.**

## Quilting Suggestion

MY HEART BELONGS TO CHOCOLATE was stitched in the ditch using invisible thread.

Bind quilt with dark red binding, following the instructions on page 10.

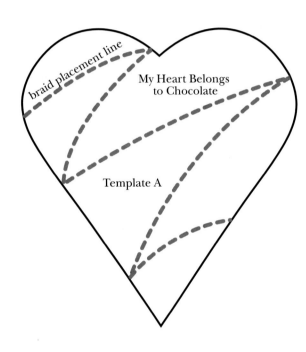

braid placement line

My Heart Belongs to Chocolate

Template A

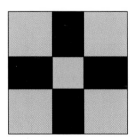

**Fig. 8.**

**Fig. 9.**

**Fig. 10.**

**Fig. 11.**

# Resources

Thank you to The Warm Company, RJR Fashion Fabrics, Benartex, Robert Kaufman Fabrics, Bali Fabrics, P&B Fabrics, Kreinik Thread, Coats and Clarks, Ami Simms, and Sew/Fit for the use of their wonderful products.

**Chocolate facts provided by:**
National Confectioners Assoc.
Chocolate Manufacturers Assoc.
7900 Westpark Blvd.
Suite A 320
McLean, VA 22102
www.candyusa.org

**Other designs**
**by Janet Jones Worley**
www.QuiltPatternsEtc.com

## FABRICS

Quilts featuring fabrics from the following manufacturers are listed below their contact information.

As you contact these manufacturers, ask for their coordinated fabric lines.

**Bali Fabrics**
554 3rd Street West
Sonoma, CA, 95476
www.balifab.com
e-mail: batik@balifab.com
CHOCOLATE COVERED CHERRIES

**Benartex, Inc.**
1460 Broadway, 8th Floor
New York, NY 10036
212-840-3250
www.Benartex.com
BLUEBERRIES & WHITE CHOCOLATE
EASTER CANDY
MY HEART BELONGS TO CHOCOLATE
SPRINKLES
STRAWBERRY CRÈME CENTERS

**P & B Fabrics, Inc.**
1580 Gilbreth Road
Burlingame, CA 94010
www.pbtex.com
BLACK FOREST

**RJR Fashion Fabrics**
13748 South Gramercy Place
Gardena, CA 90249
800-422-5426
www.rjrfabrics.com
CRÈME DE MINT
HOT CHOCOLATE

**Robert Kaufman Co., Inc.**
129 West 132nd Street
Los Angeles, CA 90061
800-877-2066
CHOCOLATE STIPPLED CHEESECAKE
JELLY BEANS
LA CHOCOLADA!

**QUILT KITS** – selected from
*Quilts for Chocolate Lovers*

**Ladyfingers Sewing Studio**
P.O. Box 3
800 Limekiln Road
Limekiln, PA 19535
Phone: 610-689-0068
fax: 610-689-4713
e-mail: ladybernina@hotmail.com
BLUEBERRIES & WHITE CHOCOLATE
EASTER CANDY
MY HEART BELONGS TO CHOCOLATE
SPRINKLES

**AUTHOR'S PREFERENCES**
**The Warm Company**
954 East Union Street
Seattle WA 98122
800-234-9276
100% cotton batting & fusible web
Warm & Natural Batting
Steam-A-Seam2

**CUTTING & SEWING MATERIALS**
**Sew/Fit Company**
5310 W. 66th Street, Unit A
Bedford Park, IL 60638-6302
708-458-5600
Add-a-Table
Rotary cutter, mat and
6½"-wide ruler

**THREAD**
**COATS & CLARK**
4135 South Stream Blvd.
Charlotte, NC 28217
704-329-5012

**METALLIC THREAD, RIBBON**
**& BRAID**
**Kreinik Metallic Threads**
3106 Timanus Lane, Suite 101
Baltimore, MD 21244
800-354-4255
www.kreinik.com
BLUEBERRIES & WHITE CHOCOLATE
#4 very fine Midnight #060
1/16" ribbon
Bahama Blue #329
Med. #16 braid
Royal Blue #033
1/8" ribbon, Star Blue #94
1/16" ribbon, Blue Ice #1432
1/8" ribbon, Silver Night #393
MY HEART BELONGS TO CHOCOLATE
1/8" braid #201C
1/8" braid #032

**PHOTO TRANSFER MATERIALS**
**Ami Simms**
**Photos-To-Fabric**
**Mallery Press, LLC**
4206 Sheraton Drive
Flint, MI 48532-3557
Toll free: 1-800-278-4824
fax: (810) 230-1516
e-mail: MalleryPress@aol.com
www.mallerypress.com

**BIAS BARS**
**Celtic Design Company**
P.O. Box 2643
Sunnyvale, CA 94087-0643
BLUEBERRIES & WHITE CHOCOLATE
#1 set, ¼" metal bias bars

**DESIGN INSPIRATION**
**Lucy Fazely Designs**
www.LucyFazely.com

**CUSTOM MACHINE QUILTING**
**Calliope Quiltworks**
115 Portal Lane
Madison, AL  35758
Beardgl@JUNO.com

**Classic Quilts**
115 Canoebrook Lane
Huntsville, AL  35806
www.classic-quilts.com

# About the Author

Janet Jones Worley is a professional quilter, quilt designer, author, and teacher. Many of her designs have been published by *McCall's Quilting, McCall's Quick Quilts, Traditional Quilter, Quick and Easy Crafts,* and House of White Birches publications. Janet also has a quilt on permanent display in the library of Peking, China.

Janet's website, www.QuiltPatternsEtc.com, features her quilt designs and offers online tutoring. While Janet loves designing, her first love is teaching. Her light-hearted approach to quilting makes her classes fun and exciting. She firmly believes that all quilters go to heaven, and that chocolate is a necessary ingredient to sustain life!

Many of Janet's designs can be seen in national and international quilt trade shows featuring Kaufman Fine Fabrics, P & B Textiles, RJR Fashion Fabrics, Benartex, David Textiles, Roc-Lon, Warm & Natural Batting, and Kreinik Metallic Threads.

# Other AQS Books

This is only a small selection of the books available from the American Quilter's Society. AQS books are known worldwide for timely topics, clear writing, beautiful color photos, and accurate illustrations and patterns. The following books are available from your local bookseller, quilt shop, or public library.

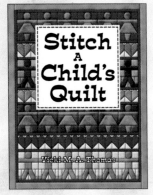

#5236          US$18.95

#5710          US$19.95

#5755          US$21.95

#5708          US$22.95

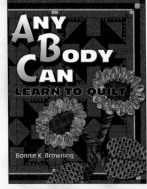

#5705          US$22.95

#5737          US$15.95

#5756          US$19.95

#5759          US$19.95

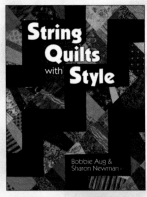

#5211          US$18.95

**Look for these books nationally or call** 1-800-626-5420